"A sensational piece of performance art, one that acknowledges theater tradition and pushes it forward as well."

—**BRUCE WEBER**, *The New York Times*

"What kind of musical is this? A fresh, unique, original, impudent, colorful, exciting, irreverent, surprising and wonderful musical, that's all!" —**REX REED**, *The New York Observer*

"Who would have thought that a 1999 Fringe Festival curiosity about ecological disaster, overpopulation and the right to pee would even make it to Broadway, let alone receive ten Tony nominations? . . . Kotis and Hollmann [have] proven that originality and irreverence can thrive on the Great White Way."

—**JASON ZINOMAN**, *TimeOut New York*

"Of course, you're not supposed to like that title—that's part of the big, good-natured, and remarkably successful joke that is *Urinetown*. A terrifically spirited sendup of musicals and their conventions." —**NANCY FRANKLIN**, *The New Yorker*

"One of the more original musicals to come along in a long time. The brilliant songs develop the story of corporate oppression and popular revolt and comment on the play itself, in hilariously sardonic homages to the Brecht-Weill canon, upbeat swing numbers and rousing spirituals."

—**ROBERT HURWITT**, *San Francisco Chronicle*

URINETOWN: THE MUSICAL

GREG KOTIS and MARK HOLLMANN

GREG KOTIS is a veteran of the Neo-Futurists, creators of the long-running, ongoing attempt to perform thirty plays in sixty minutes, *Too Much Light Makes the Baby Go Blind*. *Jobey and Katherine*, his play about fish, toast, and a love stronger and grimmer than death, enjoyed runs in New York and Chicago in 1997. As a member of the Cardiff Giant Theater Company, he appeared in countless anarchic improvisations and co-authored six plays, including *LBJFKKK*, *Love Me*, and *Aftertaste! (the Musical)*. He holds a BA in political science from the University of Chicago, and lives in Brooklyn with his wife, Ayun Halliday, and their children, India and Milo.

MARK HOLLMANN is a former ensemble member of the Cardiff Giant Theater Company in Chicago. He also played trombone for the Chicago art-rock band Maestro Subgum and the Whole, and played piano for the Second City National Touring Company and Chicago City Limits. He attended the Making Tuners Workshop at New Tuners Theatre in Chicago and the BMI Lehman Engel Musical Theatre Workshop in New York. A member of the Dramatists Guild and ASCAP, he lives in Manhattan with his wife, Jillian.

URINETOWN

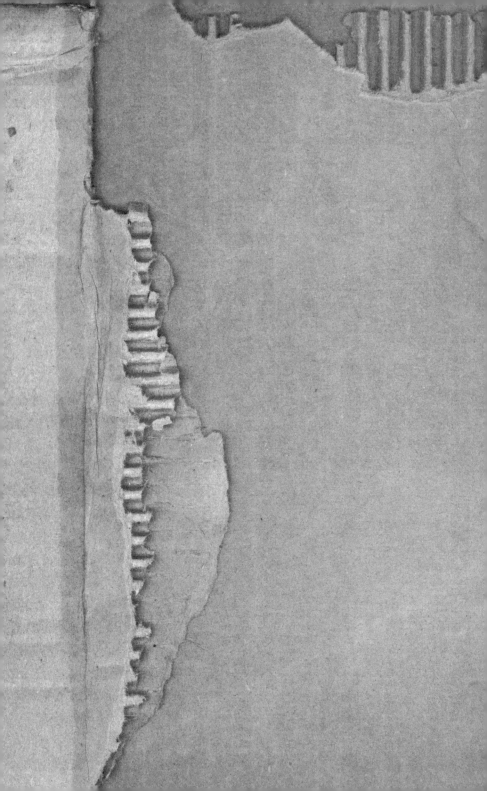

URINETOWN
THE MUSICAL

Book and lyrics by
GREG KOTIS

Music and lyrics by
MARK HOLLMANN

FABER AND FABER, INC.
An affiliate of Farrar, Straus and Giroux / New York

For Bob, Scott, Laura, Phil, Hannah, and Johnnie

FABER AND FABER, INC.
An affiliate of Farrar, Straus and Giroux
19 Union Square West, New York 10003

Libretto copyright © 1998 by Greg Kotis and Mark Hollmann
Book copyright © 2003 by Greg Kotis and Mark Hollmann
Preface copyright © 2003 by David Auburn
Introduction copyright © 2003 by Greg Kotis and Mark Hollmann
All rights reserved
Distributed in Canada by Douglas & McIntyre Ltd.
Printed in the United States of America
FIRST EDITION, 2003

Library of Congress Cataloging-in-Publication Data
Kotis, Greg.
   [Urinetown. Libretto]
   Urinetown, the musical / book by Greg Kotis ; lyrics by Greg Kotis and Mark
Hollmann.— 1st ed.
     p. cm.
   ISBN-13: 978-0-571-21182-1
   ISBN-10: 0-571-21182-8 (pbk.)
   1. Musical—Librettos.   I. Hollman, Mark, 1963–   II. Title.

ML50.K8785 U75 2002
782.1'4'0268—dc21

                                2002033875

Designed by Gretchen Achilles

www.fsgbooks.com

15 14 13 12 11 10 9 8

Theater production costs are skyrocketing everywhere, and in New York, Broadway budgets and "development" expenses can approach those of the movies. But storefront theater companies can still thrive in Chicago. Or at least they could in the late 1980s and early 1990s, when a company with drive and its own sensibility could reasonably hope to attract the attention of the public and find a space cheap enough to put on a few shows a year without going broke.

A group called Cardiff Giant found two such spaces. One was on Chicago's North Side, where they performed original plays that they wrote as an ensemble. The other was in Jimmy's Woodlawn Tap, a South Side bar not far from the University of Chicago, from which most of the group's members had either graduated or not-quite-graduated. Here they mounted a weekly improvisational show that often generated raw material for the plays.

The improv was more anarchic, the plays highly structured, but in both settings the group created a theatrical landscape with features not to be found elsewhere.

The stories were usually set in a kind of mid-twentieth-century Everytown. They were highly referential, with elements drawn impulsively from old movies, cartoons, dimly remembered TV ads and grade-school educational films, and texts from the required U. of C. humanities and sociology classes. There was a lot of intrigue, scheming, double-dealing. There were a lot of evil or demented geniuses (I remember one who derived his schemes from talking to a peanut), wise waifs (usually played by men), angry mobs, corrupt politicians, and ingenues who turned out to be as obsessive and bent as the villains they were opposing. There were copious flashbacks, flash-forwards, dream and fantasy sequences, visitations from ghosts, etc. Characters even in realistic situations supplied their own sound effects. Plot twists or surprise revelations occasioned huge double takes, accompanied by a baffled "Wha—?"

The shows were dizzying and incredibly funny. I remember many nights walking out of Jimmy's with my face aching from laughing so hard.

Anyone who has seen *Urinetown* will be familiar with that sensation. Greg Kotis and Mark Hollmann, the show's authors, were two of the driving forces behind Cardiff Giant, and for those of us who saw their Chicago shows ten or more years ago, part of the excitement of *Urinetown* is in seeing that anarchic, bizarre, Chicago storefront sensibility transferred intact, and in some ways enhanced, to the world of the big-budget Broadway musical.

This is something Broadway badly needs. Much of the energy in any art form in any era is supplied by the experiments that bubble up from below. Not very much that's new or exciting has bubbled up in the Broadway musical during the last few years, probably because of high production costs and the aesthetic conservatism they engender.

Urinetown's success is a terrific blow to that conservatism. And audiences walking out of the show on Broadway are so giddy and happy that its success there now seems like a forgone conclusion.

But of course it wasn't at first, not any more than it was obvious a decade ago that Cardiff Giant's peculiar style could work in the mainstream. It certainly wasn't obvious to me. Though I loved the shows, my memory of them isn't particularly sunny. They could be pretty bleak, actually. They put human corruption, weakness, and cupidity on hilarious display. Villains were sometimes punished, but idealism was usually betrayed, not rewarded. The overall effect was oddly, and gratifyingly, hard-headed.

This sensibility, too, is intact in *Urinetown*. What's most star-tling about the musical might be the rigor with which Kotis and Hollmann work through their famously absurd premise. The water shortage that drives the plot produces villains and heroes, corruption and idealism—but the heroes have no monopoly on virtue, and it's not just the villains who grow corrupt. Though *Urinetown* mocks the conventions of musicals, it is not primarily a spoof of them, as many reviews have held it to be (actually, it has the most solid, old-fashioned construction of any book musical in recent memory). If it is any kind of satire, it's not of musical theater but of human corruption—as Cardiff Giant's work was, and Ben Jonson's and Brecht's as well.

Like Brecht, Kotis and Hollmann hammered out a unique sensibility for themselves by performing in bars and tiny theaters. Then they refined and enlarged it to the point where it can en-tertain and speak meaningfully to a large audience. That accom-plishment doesn't just put them in a great theatrical tradition. It gives hope to storefront theater companies everywhere—and to Broadway, too.

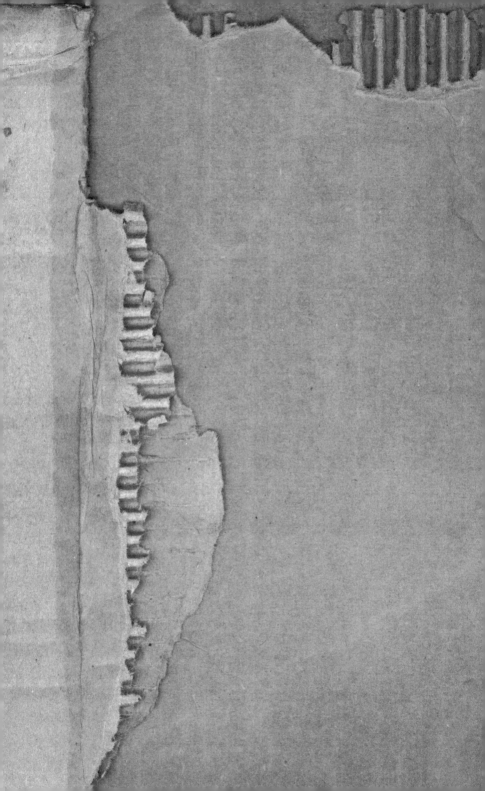

I

JUNE 2

On June 2, 2002, *Urinetown* won three Tony Awards (one for book, one for score, and a third for direction), an event that—as of this writing—still feels quite warm and wonderful and difficult to believe. Throughout the evening of the Tony broadcast, people would approach me and ask, "Did you ever think the show would get this far?" to which I would answer, "Well, no, I didn't." An obvious answer to an obvious question. *Urinetown*, as they knew, and as you may know, arrived on Broadway as a ludicrous, harebrained transfer from Off-Broadway, itself an even more ludicrous transfer from Off-Off-Broadway. The show, apparently, was this absurdist musical about a world where people had to pay to pee, appropriate, perhaps, for some fringe festival on the Lower East Side of New York City, but not for Broadway, and certainly not as a nominee for a bevy of Tony Awards. At each leg of *Urinetown*'s journey from Stanton Street (Off-Off-Broadway) to Forty-third Street (Broadway), the conventional wisdom seemed to mutter, "This must not happen." And yet, at each leg, it did happen—the show survived, flourished even, and eventually snuck its way forward toward that Broadway night of nights. By the end of the evening's festivities, these "Did you ever think?" exchanges became something of a ritual, the asker knowing the answer, the answerer welcoming the basically rhetorical question. They took on the verbal equivalent of pinching yourself to see if you're awake—"Am I dreaming? Apparently not." The question, to be sure, is still welcome, because the journey isn't over yet. As of this writing, *Urinetown* is planning a national tour, as well as a flurry of international productions, including Seoul, Tokyo, London, and more. *Urinetown* has its very own original cast recording, produced by a large, monopolizing corporation like RCA/Victor, no less. And now the text of the play has been published by a not quite monopolizing, but at least respected, mid-sized publishing outfit like Faber & Faber, complete with an introduction engaging enough to keep the reader reading until this very sentence. Given the origins and original intentions of the play, it all still feels quite difficult to believe, as well as warm and wonderful.

THE IDEA FOR *URINETOWN*

The idea for *Urinetown* first came to me during what might generously be described as a poorly planned trip to Europe during the late winter/early spring of 1995. At the time, I was performing with the Neo-Futurists, a Chicago-based experimental theater company that was taking part in a theater festival in a small Transylvanian (believe it or not) town called Sibiu. On our return flight, I decided to extend an overnight layover in Paris to spend two weeks bumming around Western Europe by myself, to see the sights, and also to try and decide whether I would propose to my girlfriend and fellow Neo-Futurist, Ayun Halliday. For some reason I thought $300 would cover my expenses, and as you might expect, I ran out of money almost immediately. What I had intended to be a meditative, economy-style backpacker excursion through the capitals of France, Germany, England, and Spain quickly devolved into a grim test of endurance, where the defining questions changed from "Am I getting enough culture?" and "How do I really feel about Ayun?" to simply "How can I not spend any money until I can reclaim my ticket to the States and go home?" For me, the answer involved sleeping in train stations, eating cheap but belly-filling foods, and, strangely enough, avoiding going to the bathroom as much as possible. Public bathrooms in Europe are pay-per-use. Some are old buildings in parks complete with towel-distributing attendants; some are state-of-the-art, self-cleaning toilet-pods set proudly near city crossroads. Each involves a fee of some kind, some more expensive than others, all at the time prohibitive to me. I have never been able to just pee in the bushes (or between parked cars, as is often done in New York), nor do I do well under the hostile gaze of restaurateurs who know a bathroom free-loader when they see one. For me, the pay-per-use amenities were it. And so it was that on one particularly cold and rainy afternoon in Paris, while I was making my way past the Luxembourg Gardens, trying to determine how badly I needed to go to the bathroom and whether I should splurge and use one of the toilet-pods I could see looming in the distance (or wait until just before dinner when I could combine two trips into one), that the notion of a city where all public amenities in town were controlled by a single malevolent, monopolizing corporation came to me. And not only would the corporation control all the public bathrooms but, being malevolent and monopolizing, it would somehow ensure the prohibition of private toilets, thus guaranteeing a steady flow of customers to its overpriced comfort stations. With its wealth and influence on the rise, it would pay off politicians and the police, outlaw going in the bushes (and between parked cars), and generally employ all available tools of persuasion to maintain its hammerlock on power. At its head would be an evil capitalist genius controlling the world from behind his corporate desk. But would he really be so evil? For the world he was controlling was suffering from a nearly uncontrollable ecological disaster—a drought that, at the beginning of our story, had already entered its twentieth year. I stood there on the sidewalk for a moment or two, thinking the thing through. The notion seemed like a patently awful one, grand and ridiculous, a career (such as it was) ending embarrassment. And yet, at its core, it would also be a grand, ridiculous reflection of the world as we know it to be, complete with rich and poor, the powerful and the powerless, a government controlled by industry and an industry that exists apart from and above us all. And driving it all would be the disaster, in this case the drought, a fact that trumped all the other facts: the love, the rage, the greed, everything. It would be a musical, yes, a very big musical, and it would be called *Urinetown*. It might not be performed, perhaps should not be performed, but it would be called *Urinetown*, and it would take place in a town where everybody had to pay to pee. Such is the thinking that comes from being too homesick, too broke, and too full of belly-filling foods, while inhibiting natural bodily functions for too long.

MARK

Upon returning to the United States and moving to New York City (with Ayun, then my fiancée) to continue performing with the Neo-Futurists, I approached Mark Hollmann, a long-time friend and past collaborator, and pitched the idea to him. Strangely, he was interested. Mark and I had worked intensively years before with the Cardiff Giant Theater Company, creating new plays with other company members through a process of ensemble improvisation. Since then, Mark had moved to New York to pursue a career as a composer while I stayed in Chicago to continue working with the Neo-Futurists, among other companies. Initially, I presented Mark with a narrative skeleton and a few scenes. Mark took the material away and came back a few weeks later with "It's a Privilege to Pee," Penelope Pennywise's Act I wail about the cold, hard facts of life during the drought. It was angry, pained, an unapologetic march in the tradition of Brecht-Weill. There was Ms. Pennywise laying down the law to the downtrodden, screaming the truth as she knew it, an absurdist Brechtian anti-heroine. The show came alive in Mark's new song, the colors were clear, the tone pitch-perfect.

Over the next three years we met after services at a church where Mark played organ, sometimes infrequently, sometimes intensively, trading notes and sharing the progress we had made in the intervening weeks. The process was slow, unpredictable, a task of exploring the metaphor to its utmost, trying to bring the world of the play into view. At first it was difficult to believe we were putting so much energy into this show called *Urinetown*; it was a freak show of a musical, a Frankenstein's Monster best kept in the basement. We wrote it as if we didn't expect anyone but maybe a few friends to see it, because at first we really didn't expect anyone but maybe a few friends to see it. We ballooned the cast size out to thirty-six, a comfortably unworkable crowd of actors no producer would ever agree to (if ever one were to agree to our premise in the first place). We devised a ghastly ending where Cladwell's potbelly (he was originally described as a portly man) was revealed to be an obscenely distended bladder strapped to his body with belts, an unforgivably vulgar costume requirement we felt confident no one could build. We hobbled our monster, sabotaging it with unproducible choices that would keep the work safely off the stage and in our respective desk drawers, where it belonged. And yet, at the same time, the madness of the thing felt strangely joyful and free. Since it was unproducible, we allowed ourselves complete liberty in imagining the play, making choices that were not just bad for the sake of being bad but reckless for the sake of seeing where a story goes when it goes where it probably shouldn't. What happens if the hero dies, not heroically, but desperately, and alone with his enemies? What happens if the heroine is allowed her anger, then allowed to act upon her impulse to incite a mob to murder her father? And what happens if the play offers no clear prescription for the troubles it imagines, no "Love is the answer" or "Be true to yourself and all will be well"? And here we found the real heart of the play, the sense of fear that had hovered over all our efforts. What had been a vague, uncertain point of view came into sharper relief for us as the play grew bloodier and the stakes of the story rose.

I have never been an environmentalist in any productive sense, nor can I claim to be a social activist, nor would I describe myself as a particularly good citizen. But at the same time, I (like most Americans, I suspect) have this creeping sense of dread that we're in the process of doing ourselves in, slowly but steadily, and there's nothing we can do about it. We burn too much oil, build too many roads and too many houses, create too much garbage, and as human beings interested in pleasure, convenience, personal freedom, and individual progress, we're simply incapable of making the changes necessary to save ourselves. The evidence seems to be everywhere, in the oddness of recent climate swings, in estimates of future population growth, and in the choice of leaders we select to articulate our national response to these facts. These problems seem so huge, so complete, so fundamental as to be unsolvable, and that was the issue Mark and I ultimately hoped to consider with this play. Yes, *Urinetown* would be absurd, allegorical, ridiculous, unproducible. But, at the same time, it would present a world long past the point where good intentions could do any good, a future we both fear and anticipate in this world, silently for the most part. And perhaps a musical that had deliberately shed the traditional credentials of a happy ending, or even a decent title, might be exactly the right play to present the thought we had in mind. We shrunk the cast down to sixteen, then fifteen. We discovered the true ending of the play, one that kept our villain a human being. And (unproducible choices aside) we stayed true to the formal rules of musical theater writing as best we could, wondering whether they might apply even to *Urinetown*.

THE FRINGE FESTIVAL

Mark and I spent the second half of 1998 dutifully sending out first draft scripts and demo tapes to theaters, agents, and producers around the country, who would then dutifully send form letters back to us in response. Our roots were in the do-it-yourself theater world, but our hope was to find an ally in more established circles who could help us put our monster on its feet. Unfortunately (or fortunately, as it turned out), our unproducible choices proved entirely convincing, and by April 1999 we had exhausted all traditional avenues of production and/or development save for an impoverished, upstart theater festival that took place each August in Manhattan called the New York International Fringe Festival. The Fringe, to be sure, was a last resort for us. As Mark and I well knew, the Fringe was not so much a festival as a barely controlled riot where as many as 150 theater productions from across the country and around the world descended on the streets of the Lower East Side for ten days in August, each working ferociously to press-gang as many audience members as they could find to see their show. What we had in mind was a musical, a real musical, that most intricate piece of theatrical machinery, and to trust it to the certain anarchy of the Fringe Festival seemed like folly. But by April 1999 it was the Fringe Festival or nothing, and while we toyed with nothing, we settled on the Fringe. Lucky for us.

Fired anew by the threat of impending production, Mark and I worked through the spring, meeting evenings and weekends in the church where Mark played organ to polish the script into rehearsal readiness. We assembled an intrepid cast of young performers, each stuck in New York for the summer for various reasons, but each game enough to give our show a shot. We rehearsed whenever we could (also in Mark's church), our director tripling as choreographer and musical director, our assistant director quadrupling as prop master, stage manager, and all-round chief of staff. Mark and I polished the script further, and day by day, the show was whipped, cajoled, and coddled into shape. Our last night in the church we performed a run-through for a few of our friends. They were polite and encouraging, some congratulatory, some quietly but quite obviously concerned for our future. That performance constituted our invited dress rehearsal and entire preview process rolled into one. We were exhausted and terrified, but it began to seem like we had something approximating a show.

Fringe Festival rules allowed each production one eight-hour period for a technical rehearsal to tech its show in its assigned theater. In both our theater assignment and our tech time we got two extremely lucky breaks. Our theater, a converted garage on the corner of Stanton and Ridge, was immediately next door to where festival tickets were sold, and noon to eight (our tech time) proved to be an extremely busy shift. As we rehearsed, ticket sellers, attracted by the sounds being made next door, would drift in to see who was singing, and why. And as ticket buyers began showing up and asking the sellers for guidance, word spread that the festival was hosting a musical this year, a real musical with singing and everything. Advance sales picked up.

The theater was very hot for our first performance, as it would be for all performances. The roof of the garage was one vast, tar-covered expanse that absorbed and exaggerated all the heat of the August sun. Fans were brought in and spread throughout the house, hung from the ceilings, all humming loudly, moving the hot air around. A garage door on the side of the theater was kept open to let in fresh air, which also let in chatter from the ticket booths. It was a dirty, dangerous, uncomfortable place to see a show, let alone perform one, and all in all the perfect place to present *Urinetown*. Audience members streamed in, stepping over extension cords and onto shaky risers to find their seats. I hovered in the catwalks above the back of the house, chewing my cuticles, trying to read the audience. Then Mark, our entire orchestra, began to play his overture on a single upright piano placed just house left of the stage. The crowd grew quiet, curious. The lights went down, the cast took their positions, and Jay Rhoderick, our Officer Lockstock for the Fringe production, entered from the house and began talking to the audience. As quiet as the audience was, they grew quieter still; an actor dressed as a policeman was addressing them from the stage. There are many kinds of silence in theater, some good, some not so good. This was a good silence, an alert silence—they were paying attention. As Jay spoke, a dirge-like, mournful hymn filled the garage, complete with part singing and full-chorus chords. This, apparently, was not what the audience had expected to hear, not at the Fringe Festival, and certainly not from a show called *Urinetown*. They listened harder. Then they started to laugh. Lines were dropped throughout that first performance, cues were missed, props were fumbled, the heat in the theater actually rose, pushed up by all the lighting instruments working at once, but we were getting laughs. The crowd, our first crowd, was with us. When the lights popped off at the end of the first-act finale, the audience leaped to its feet; they cheered. Mark sat in a pool of sweat by his piano, unsure of how we had done, still peering at his sheet music, reliving his errors. The cast mingled backstage, their costumes sopping wet with perspiration, exhausted but happy to be through the first half. And this is how we began. *Urinetown* was performed eight times as part of the Fringe, and four more times at the same theater the weekend after the festival closed. We oversold nearly every performance, garnered the kind of critical response you inevitably daydream about working in theater, and had a good time in the process. Even then we were being asked, "Did you ever think the show would get this far?"

DEAL WITH THE DEVIL

Of all the industry people who wandered through our show, it was only the Araca Group, partnered by Mike Rego, Matthew Rego, and Hank Unger, who understood how far *Urinetown* might one day go, and how it could get there. Mike, Matthew, and Hank were upstarts, buccaneering producers eager for a horse to bet on, and fully willing to risk other people's money (as well as their own) on a long shot like *Urinetown*. When I first met Mike, he struck me as the enemy incarnate (albeit a very young one), acutely interested in money, ambitious, strangely good-looking, and not ashamed to interrupt our conversation to answer his cellphone. At our initial meeting on the night that he first saw the show, Mike mostly asked questions, keeping his cards close to his chest, his enthusiasm muted. Whom had we talked to? What were our plans? How committed were we to the material? The director? The cast? He liked the show. He was busy. He'd let us know. It was one of several meetings we "took" (as we learned to say) during and immediately after the Fringe, vaguely promising, but also vaguely dispiriting. Our first choice was to remount the show as it was, a raw and rebellious production that might run in some other garage for a while, albeit a nicer one. But the more we talked to prospective producers, the more unlikely that particular prospect seemed to be. Space was scarce, money was scarce, and real musicals were impossible enough to produce, let alone the deliberately impossible one we hoped to remount. Months passed, and by the time the Araca Group called us in for a second meeting, Mark and I had already exhausted the various VIPs we had courted since the Fringe production had closed, each well-intentioned but ultimately in no position to advance our cause.

The proposal the Araca Group made to us was this: Bring in a new director, someone known and respected, open casting to a wider pool of talent including seasoned veterans, and see what happens when the material is put in front of the powers that be. As a young and relatively green producing outfit, Araca was in a position to mount the show as a staged reading, but not much more. The purpose of the reading would be to test the material away from the Fringe environment, and to solicit the interest and assistance of more experienced producing partners with greater resources and know-how. The show is an odd duck, they argued, but treat it like a Broadway musical and it might just have legs. This, of course, was the hardest part of our journey with the show. We felt loyal and indebted to our Fringe group, and never before in our time writing plays had we been asked to consider recasting anything. Shows were done with friends for the love of it as much as anything else; changing the roster defeated the purpose of the thing. But Araca's argument was strong: Let backers see this material with actors they trusted and its potential (or lack thereof) would be apparent. We lobbied for our cast, demanding they all get a shot in front of the new director, hoping for the best. In the end, our choice was to trust the play to the Araca Group or walk away from the show for good. We considered walking away, but in the end we chose to trust them.

RANDO & CO.

Unbeknownst to us, the Araca Group knew only one director of note—John Rando—and with him we received perhaps the luckiest break of all. In our first meeting with John he spoke seriously, gravely even, about the substance of the play, its historical antecedents, its larger context. He spoke to no one in particular, to a spot hovering about three inches above the center of the conference table we had spread ourselves around. But as he spoke he would crack up from time to time, shake off the grimness for a second with an image of ridiculousness he hoped to see in the show, then continue, grim again. Here was the man for the job, serious and loopy at the same time. John was then joined by the musical director Edward Strauss, grim and loopy in his own way, but exacting in precisely the way a musical director needed to be with our material.

Over the next two months we collected a cast and set about mounting what's known as a twenty-hour reading. Two Fringe cast members were invited, including Spencer Kayden, who would continue with the production to Broadway, a happy vote of confidence to the old crew, a crucial aesthetic clue to the new one. What's special about a twenty-hour reading is that the actors don't have to be paid that much (good for the producers, bad for the actors), but only twenty hours of their time can be used from the first moment of rehearsal to the final moment of the reading (good for the actors, bad for the producers—and the writers, I suppose). A stopwatch was present continuously, actors were stopped and released mid-sentence to keep the schedule on schedule; a near-panicky feverishness hovered over most of the proceedings. But as constrained as the process was, this was Mark's and my first real taste of the big time. Here we were, two unknowns from the do-it-yourself world of way-downtown theater, and each day we arrived at rehearsal to watch these seasoned actors and directors apply their abilities to our play. We got to offer opinions, participate in decisions, people treated us nice. And all the while, the play was coming closer and closer into view. Here was Nancy Opel belting out Penelope Pennywise's "It's a Privilege to Pee" with a mad rage and remorse above and beyond our wildest hopes. There was Jennifer Laura Thompson as Hope Cladwell, more captivating and more beautiful than the Grace Kelly her character was first modeled on, and Daniel Marcus, giddily bloodthirsty as Lockstock's sidekick, Officer Barrel. And, finally, there was Spencer as Little Sally, a friend and fellow collaborator from Neo-Futurist days, a Fringe stowaway like ourselves, holding her own with the pros.

BIG TIME

The reading was presented twice in January 2000 at New Dramatists on West Forty-fourth Street, the first during a traffic-stopping blizzard, the second two days later amid the frozen detritus left by the storm. People came slogging through the snow, important people, industry people, including Michael David and Lauren Mitchell of Dodger Theatricals. Although I didn't know it at the time, Dodger was and is one of the biggest players on Broadway. Their track record extends back decades, including *Gospel at Colonus*, *Wrong Mountain*, and many of the big-time Broadway revivals of recent years. At first glance, Michael seemed to have something of the mad Russian holy man about him, a benevolent version of Rasputin: friendly enough, but with all the spark that prerevolutionary figure suggests. And Lauren was (and is) strikingly tall and elegant, every bit the Broadway performer she began her career as. In addition to Michael and Lauren, each performance was attended by the powerful prospective producers the Araca Group had spoken of, representatives from many of the major producing organizations and performing arts institutions in the city, precisely the people Mark and I had solicited two years before.

I was sitting in my car in a small town on Long Island, days after the reading, scouting houses for the TV show *Law & Order* (my day job), when Mike Rego called to tell me the Dodgers wanted in. This was that particular piece of good fortune that made everything that followed possible. Michael and Lauren were the "powers that be," so to speak, precisely the kind of creative producers a show like *Urinetown* needed. Mark and I, as well as Mike, Matthew, and Hank, were called into a meeting at Dodger Theatricals, a high-floor office in an old-time New York building overlooking Times Square. Posters of familiar theatrical triumphs covered the walls, the office hummed (as they say) with important activity, all in all a convincing epicenter of Broadway power and accomplishment. We collected in a small conference room with clear views of New Jersey, and were offered water and coffee while we waited; then Lauren and Michael joined us, for them another stop on a busy day. They sat down, introduced themselves, and then began discussing the play as if they really meant to produce it. They liked the material. They liked the title! What was our vision for the show? The play was an Off-Broadway play, but could we imagine it on Broadway? It's difficult to understate the miracle of their enthusiasm. In a Broadway landscape that had become increasingly risk-averse and corporatized, here were two players with solid reputations offering to roll the dice and see what fate awaited those who chose to produce the unproducible play.

Months were committed to finding the right performance space, which turned out to be a poor but tenacious theater operating above an active courtroom on West Fifty-fourth Street. Weeks were spent assembling a creative team, then auditioning new cast members to join Nancy, Jennifer, Daniel, and Spencer, including David Beach, Rachel Coloff, Rick Crom, John Cullum, John Deyle, Hunter Foster, Victor W. Hawks, Ken Jennings, Megan Lawrence, Jeff McCarthy, Lawrence E. Street, Kay Walbye, and (eventually) Jennifer Cody. Weeks of rehearsals followed, a thrilling process for me. There was John Cullum, cunning and smooth, creating the villain Cladwell before our very eyes. There was Hunter Foster creating Bobby Strong, Cladwell's nemesis, giving the hero more honesty and gritty charisma than the James Dean–style character we had originally envisioned. And there was Jeff McCarthy, the keystone of all our efforts, anchoring the show as Officer Lockstock, a murderously tough cop on the take with a soft spot for a little girl who would join him in explaining the show to the audience. And he had to sing, too. Amid it all, an ensemble came into being, the creators of Tiny Tom, Hot Blades Harry, Senator Fipp, Mr. McQueen, Josephine Strong, Billy Boy Bill, Robby the Stockfish, Soupy Sue, and Little Becky Two-Shoes, a group that had to work harder, dance harder, and perform harder than seemed possible. Rewrites were requested and, after some hair pulling, delivered. Characters were discovered, gags were discovered, the show was choreographed (by the formidable John Carrafa), orchestrated (by the unrivaled Bruce Coughlin), and altogether "Broadway-fied," as a friend termed it. A few days before tech rehearsals began, we were invited to see the set design Scott Pask had installed in the theater, a stunning experience for two writers previously accustomed to dump-picked couches constituting the centerpieces of designs for past plays. More stunning still was to see Jonathan Bixby and Gregory Gale's costumes, worn on that stage by our cast and lit by Brian MacDevitt's wonderful plot. Advertisements appeared. Articles appeared. Word spread that *Urinetown* had found its way to a commercial production. How was it possible? And yet it was happening. Previews began Sunday, April 1, a presumed April Fools' joke for some. And then, finally, implausibly, *Urinetown* opened Off-Broadway, Sunday, May 6, 2001, roughly nineteen months after closing at the Fringe.

At the opening-night party at a bar near the theater, Hank Unger arrived with the *New York Times* review. In olden days people would wait for the papers to land in bundles on the sidewalk to learn what critical fate had befallen their show. Nowadays, reviews are posted first on the Internet, so that's what Hank had, a printout from the *Times*'s Web site. A few of us collected on the sidewalk outside the bar. Jeff McCarthy, our barrel-chested, silver-maned Officer Lockstock, read it aloud. In the world of New York theater every accolade is precious, but the *Times*, as the tradition goes, gives life or takes it away. In our case, we had been given life—a lot of life. *Urinetown* sold out its run, then extended performances to the end of June. The production was blessed with more accolades, including eleven Drama Desk nominations, two Obie Awards, and a berth in that season's "Best Plays" anthology. Shortly before the end of our Off-Broadway run, Mike Rego assembled the cast before a show to share with them (and with us) the outcome of the producers' private schemings. We were going to Broadway, all of us. They didn't know where, exactly, but it was happening, so get ready. There was no cheer during his announcement, no exhalation that follows the crossing of a finish line. The cast asked questions, quietly, cautiously. People tugged on their costumes, exchanging quick, happy grins. Their lives were changing. Our lives were changing. We had all bet on the right horse.

The Henry Miller, our Broadway destination, had been dark and derelict as a legitimate Broadway theater until only a few years before *Urinetown* transferred there. Ultimately resuscitated by a revival of *Cabaret*, the Henry Miller had been a nightclub, a porn house, and an otherwise uncelebrated venue for sex farces and revues since the 1960s. Previous to that, the Henry Miller had been a legitimate stage, including among its productions Eugene O'Neill's *Days Without End*, T. S. Eliot's *The Cocktail Party*, and Thornton Wilder's Pulitzer Prize–winning *Our Town*, but that heyday was long gone by the time we arrived. During our first walk-through of the space, we found the Henry Miller to be a dusty, crumbling antique, complete with holes in the ceiling and leopardskin carpeting left over from its seedier days. But like the Stanton Street garage, and the floor above the court/precinct, the Henry Miller was the perfect place for *Urinetown*. Broadway previews began Monday, August 27, adjustments being made all the while as we approached our September 13 opening. Monday, September 10, as well as Tuesday, September 11, were press nights, those specific performances critics attend in advance of a show's actual premiere. Monday's performance was strong, an evening witnessed by reviewers from *The New York Observer*, the *Newark Star-Ledger*, and *USA Today*, among others. Tuesday, September 11, was to be even more crucial, including theater writers from *Newsday*, the Associated Press, *Variety*, and *The New York Times*. That performance, of course, never took place. The planes struck in the morning, and I, like many New Yorkers, spent the day alternately hovering by the radio, looking out my window toward downtown Manhattan, and venturing into the streets of my neighborhood to try to understand what had become of our city. Broadway performances were cancelled for that evening, as they would be for the next, and as far as we knew, we wouldn't be opening for some time. It was difficult to imagine how we could possibly present our absurdist comedy in the midst of so much tragedy, confusion, and fear. But at the behest of the mayor, we did reopen, along with the rest of Broadway, inviting audiences to come back the Thursday after the attacks. Times Square was relatively empty that night, itself an antici-pated target, as it still is. Our audience was small, anxious, but eager, I think, to be in one another's company. Our director, John Rando, walked onstage and said simply that another word for life is creativity. Theater, he said, could not save lives, nor could it put out fires, but it could offer creativity and life, which is what we hoped to offer that night. John thanked the audience and walked offstage. The lights dimmed, the overture played, the actors took their places, and the show began. Theater is a poor relative in some ways to other forms of entertainment, to cinema or television. But that night, for those audience members, there could have been no greater way to spend the evening than sitting in a theater witnessing fellow New Yorkers tell a story on a stage a few feet in front of them. Whatever fears that group of theater-goers had, for themselves or their city, the actors and the musi-cians and the crew had also. But those fears were shushed away for the evening by the choice to be together, in that place, at that time.

Urinetown formally opened September 20, one week after our intended premiere. Again, the reviews were good. The critics re-minded us that there truly was a serious core to all our silliness, after all, and furthermore, silliness can be anything but unwel-come during times as serious as those we were all experiencing. Audiences grew, but each week we stayed open seemed like something of a miracle. Broadway faltered, then found its foot-ing, revived by the goodwill of the city, just as the city was re-vived by the goodwill of the country. During one week that autumn, a crowd of two hundred Oregonians arrived in New

York en masse, declaring they would do their part by spending as much money as they could, in part on theater. *Urinetown*'s cast, musicians, and crew labored week by week throughout that most difficult season, breathing life night after night into our musical with the terrible title. Houses were full, then slow, then full again. The show survived, prospered, and as the months ticked off, we drew ever closer to awards season, even becoming a contender for some of the most coveted statuettes of all. On May 6, one year to the day after opening Off-Broadway, thirty-one months after closing at the Fringe Festival, *Urinetown* was happy indeed to receive ten Tony nominations, including one for Spencer.

Greg Kotis
New York City
July 24, 2002

II

If a telephone poll had been taken on the matter, I suspect that most Americans would have said that the title alone made *Urinetown* not just a bad idea for a musical but a really terrible idea for a musical. That is, if they had not already hung up. When Greg Kotis, having invited me over to his East Ninth Street apartment in New York on a spring evening six years ago to talk about collaborating on a new musical, asked me what I thought, my answer probably placed me—with him—in a minority of two. I believed from the moment I heard it that the premise for *Urinetown* was one of the best with which I had ever been presented. Yes, the title made me nervous, but my many years in the fringe-performing-arts scene in Chicago—a background I share with Greg—had opened my small-town Midwestern boy's mind to what I once might have thought taboo.

Our shared background included many prior collaborations, through which the style of our work together on *Urinetown* can be traced (by the countless hordes I'm certain were secretly following our heretofore obscure careers). We first collaborated in the late 1980s and early 1990s, when we were both coming of age artistically in our twenties as ensemble members of the Cardiff Giant Theater Company, a now-defunct improvisational theater troupe in Chicago. As actor/playwrights in Cardiff Giant, we and our fellow ensemble members wrote, acted in, directed, and produced five full-length plays and two full-length musicals. We also performed countless improv sets, based on audience suggestions, in a weekly hour-long show called *Avant-Garfielde*.

Over the course of about seven years as an active group, Cardiff Giant developed a distinct style of dark comedy, with broad characters playing out often-absurd situations in a familiar, yet not specifically identifiable, world. Greg and I had that style in common, along with a resourcefulness and work ethic that had helped keep Cardiff Giant artistically productive in spite of a tiny budget, like so many other Chicago non-Equity theater companies. I think that Greg hoped to draw on all that when he tapped me as composer and lyricist for *Urinetown*.

In addition to working with Cardiff Giant, Greg worked with Chicago's famed Neo-Futurists troupe as a writer/performer in the long-running *Too Much Light Makes the Baby Go Blind*. I had branched out to play the trombone for Maestro Subgum and the Whole, a highly theatrical but mostly indescribable cabaret/ art-rock band. Like Cardiff Giant, these groups made up for in imagination and creativity what they lacked in funds. They engendered a definite outsider's sensibility in Greg and me, and that prepared us well for the creation of *Urinetown*.

For with our respective post–Cardiff Giant work, I can see how Greg and I were pushing our artistic tastes to new extremes. In the process, previously off-limits material (by Cardiff Giant standards) became fair game. In one of Greg's two-minute plays for *Too Much Light*, an exuberant narrator, played by Greg, explains repeatedly and in great detail how "Farts Come!" (What, you expected *roses* from the future author of *Urinetown*?) For my part, working with Maestro Subgum exposed me to a challenging new aesthetic in music and lyrics. Many of the songs we performed—written by the group's main songwriters, Beau O'Reilly, Michael Greenberg, and Jenny Magnus—dealt with heroin addiction, suicide, and other socially unacceptable behavior. These were topics that I had rarely thought or talked about, much less written songs about, but I think that performing them night after night broadened my viewpoint. It may even have prepared me to say yes to Greg Kotis when he asked me to write the songs for a musical centered on peeing.

It wasn't merely a musical centered on peeing, however. Greg's concept for *Urinetown* rose above its provocative title. The project he proposed to me had all the elements of a great musical: a love story set against the backdrop of social upheaval, a protagonist who would fight to the death for what he wanted, and a colorful cast of supporting characters. It also had the potential for comic social commentary, like the Cardiff Giant shows. Moreover, in choosing to work with each other again, Greg and I had a clear understanding that *Urinetown*, in spite of its title, would contain no swear words or off-color situations, which had been our principle in Cardiff Giant.

As composer and lyricist for our brand-new collaboration, I had two immediate tasks: to start setting a tone or style for the music of the score and to find the places in Greg's script that could be turned into songs. Although Greg eventually joined me in writing lyrics, I always felt that spotting songs was mainly my job. At this point, in the late spring of 1996, not much of a script existed, and Greg would not complete a full first draft until late 1997. From the first few pages he gave me, however, I was able to get a handle on a style and could easily spot a terrific song opportunity.

It came in a scene early in Act I, wherein we meet Penelope Pennywise, the hard-bitten matron of the filthiest urinal in town. In this moment she is reading the riot act to the downtrodden customers of her Public Amenity #9. It reminded me of a song from *Die Dreigroschenoper*, or *The Threepenny Opera*, the 1928 musical theater masterpiece by Bertolt Brecht and Kurt Weill. The song was "Der Morgenchoral des Peachum" or "The Morning Hymn of Peachum," Mr. Peachum's wake-up call to his company of beggars. Brecht's opening lyrics for Peachum, which translate as "Wake up, you rotting Christians," and which Weill set with a craftily repetitive melody and droning accompaniment, convey to me a man long convinced that the world is a fraud and wearily resigned to his place in it.

Like Ms. Pennywise, Peachum is delivering the message that all is not right in the world, and as he does, we understand that he would rather deliver this message than hear it himself. I made Pennywise's "It's a Privilege to Pee" faster and more martial than Peachum's "Morning Hymn," but the stark, unapologetically dim worldview of Peachum helped me believe that Penny's song was possible. In both cases, it is the singers' righteous duty to tell the truth as they see it, and to lay down the law, hard.

When I had finished a first draft of the music and lyrics for "It's a Privilege to Pee," I called Greg and invited him to hear it. We met at Christ Lutheran Church on East Nineteenth Street in Manhattan, where I served as organist. Sitting at the piano in the sanctuary, amid stained-glass windows depicting scenes from the Bible and tile mosaics portraying the saints, I played and sang Penny's rant, which got Greg laughing in appreciation. Laughter would become a barometer for us: if I laughed spontaneously at Greg's writing or he at mine, whatever got us laughing would usually stay in the show. That evening, I could tell from Greg's laughter that this song clicked with his vision for *Urinetown* and that we were on to something.

Although "It's a Privilege to Pee" was an early stylistic success, the entire score was not written under the influence of Weill and Brecht. I reached a certain point, perhaps after writing the "Mack the Knife"–like "Urinetown" opening number, when it became increasingly less practical to toe the line. The Brecht/Weill colors that came easily to me seemed to be a rather limited palette. I soon turned to whatever influence or model seemed appropriate for musically dramatizing the remaining spots for songs in Greg's libretto. As a Lutheran church organist, I felt competent to tackle a hymn tune in "I See a River." The melody of "Tell Her I Love Her" struck Greg and me as that of a mournful Irish ballad, well suited to Little Sally's report to her fellow revolutionaries. "Run, Freedom, Run" was a typical second-act musical-comedy gospel tune.

In spite of a laundry list of stylistic and structural influences (the ones that I'm aware of run the gamut from J. S. Bach to the B-52s), I tried to keep the score from veering into blatant parody. I based this attitude on a rule of thumb in show business: A joke is funnier if you don't smile while you're telling it. Since I felt confident that Greg's script as well as his lyric contributions covered our satirical and parodical bases, I approached the songwriting with utter seriousness and all the craft I could muster.

That craft was one I had been honing since childhood. My parents indulged me in piano lessons from the age of seven until I left home for college, where I studied music composition and decided that I wanted to write musicals for the rest of my life. After college, I had the good fortune to study musical-theater songwriting with some extremely able teachers. At the same time that I was performing in Chicago's fringe music and theater scene, I was also enrolled in the musical-theater writing workshop of John Sparks. In his classes at Theatre Building Chicago, John taught me the anatomy of a theater song, from AABA structure to how to build a comedy-song lyric so that the joke comes at the end of the line, where it packs more of a punch. When I moved to New York in 1993, I continued my studies at the BMI Lehman Engel Musical Theatre Workshop, where Skip Kennon and Richard Engquist picked up where John had left off. All during this time I was writing musicals to put these lessons into practice, so that when Greg asked me to work with him in 1996, I had been writing songs for eleven years and had completed three full-length and four one-act musicals.

This training and experience helped me follow another rule of thumb in show business while writing the score for *Urinetown*:

You have to know and respect a form thoroughly before you can satirize it. At our Sunday writing sessions, when we sat around the piano at the church, I remember feeling that I was serving as the musical theater expert for our collaboration. Greg had never seen a musical on Broadway, whereas I had studied the form for some time, and I often found myself suggesting that we turn to the exemplar American musicals for guidance.

Some of those guiding principles were specific; others were more general. One instance of a specific principle would be the appeal of a rousing second-act gospel number. Broadway musicals provide examples, from Frank Loesser ("Sit Down, You're Rockin' the Boat" from *Guys and Dolls*, 1950) to Frank Wildhorn ("River Jordan" from *The Civil War*, 1999). *Urinetown's* score copies this template with the aforementioned "Run, Freedom, Run."

Then there was a moment later in the second act, after "Run, Freedom, Run," when I turned to a more general principle for help. It was the point in the story when the rebel poor take to the streets for revenge. We had already attempted to dramatize it musically with a slow, spooky reprise of "Tell Her I Love Her" that ended up falling flat. In trying to figure out why the reprise failed, I realized that its lugubriousness doomed it. The show needed a jolt of energy at this juncture, not eerie reflection. I was reminded of George Gershwin's comment that just as an army travels on its stomach, musicals travel on two-four (quick tempo) time. That anecdote became the inspiration for the late-second-act production number/montage "We're Not Sorry," which is anything but lugubrious.

While I thought I had all the answers based on my love of old musicals, I soon learned, when I submitted a draft of the love ballad "Follow Your Heart" to Greg, that simply following those old paradigms wouldn't be enough to make the show work. He quickly sensed that something was amiss with the number. I had written a thoroughly sincere, straightforward ballad for the young lovers, Bobby and Hope, right out of the musical-comedy playbook. Its lyrics were earnest and its melody was bittersweet. Greg loved the melody, but asked for a crack at rewriting some of the lyrics. He came back with one of the surest laughs in the show when Bobby sings:

> *Someday I'll meet someone*
> *Whose heart joins with mine,*
> *Aortas and arteries all intertwined.*
> *They'll beat so much stronger*
> *Than they could apart.*
> *Eight chambers of muscle to hustle*
> *The love in our heart.*

As a result of Greg's lyric rewrite and his interweaving of the lovers' dialogue amid verses of the song, we ended up with a musical scene that walks a tightrope between comedy and storybook romance. The song and situation make us laugh, yet they also lead us to discover that we can care about Bobby and Hope. The process of arriving at the final version of "Follow Your Heart" exemplifies a push-and-pull between tradition and insurgence that made our collaboration unique in my experience.

In June 1998, after several months of Sunday writing sessions at the church, I at the piano with my music paper, Greg sprawled out on the altar steps nearby with his notepad, and both of us with our rhyming dictionaries and thesauruses on hand, we had a complete first draft with songs.

The teachers in my musical-theater writing workshops had encouraged me to think in terms of professional productions for my work. Armed with information and advice from Dramatists Guild newsletters and *The Dramatists Sourcebook*, I suggested to

Greg that we aggressively market *Urinetown* to potential producers and agents. I believed so strongly in the material that I was confident it would be worth the effort.

Over a hundred rejection letters later (ranging from polite brush-off to the more insistent please-don't-contact-us-again brush-off), our Chicago fringe do-it-yourself background gave us the practical experience we needed to produce *Urinetown* ourselves at the 1999 New York International Fringe Festival, also known as FringeNYC. Any disappointment we felt at the utter failure of our attempt to break into the world of legitimate theater with *Urinetown* would turn out to have been premature. At FringeNYC, to our great surprise, *Urinetown* met with immediate success. Soon Greg and I found that our minority of two was growing. We went from packed houses Off-Off-Broadway at our FringeNYC venue on Stanton Street to an Off-Broadway production at the American Theatre of Actors in May 2001, and finally, improbably, to Broadway's Henry Miller Theatre in September 2001.

I will never forget the sound, at the first Broadway preview, of six hundred people laughing at one of Greg's lines at the start of Act I. Since Chicago storefront theaters typically seat only sixty or seventy people, neither of us had ever heard that large an audience appreciating our writing. It was a thrilling vindication of Greg's vision. It was also the first overwhelming sign we had that, if polled, even Broadway was willing to say a resounding YES to *Urinetown*.

Mark Hollmann
Paris
July 24, 2002

URINETOWN

Originally produced by Theater of the Apes and presented in August 1999 by the New York International Fringe Festival, a production of the Present Company. Directed by Joseph P. McDonnell. Stage manager: Michael Stuart; assistant director / prop design: Wylie Goodman; costume design: Karen Flood; lighting: Peggotty Roecker; scene design: Jane Charlotte Jones.

CAST OF CHARACTERS IN THE FRINGE FESTIVAL PRODUCTION

OFFICER LOCKSTOCK	Jay Rhoderick
LITTLE SALLY	Spencer Kayden
BOBBY STRONG	Wilson Hall
HOPE CLADWELL	Louise Rozett
CALDWELL B. CLADWELL	Adam Grant
PENELOPE PENNYWISE	Carol Hickey
OFFICER BARREL	Victor Khodadad
MR. MCQUEEN	Rob Maitner
SENATOR FIPP	Terry Cosentino
OLD MAN STRONG	Nick Balaban
JOSEPHINE STRONG	Kristen Anderson
HOT BLADES HARRY	Nick Balaban
SOUPY SUE	Bellavia Mauro
TINY TOM	Zachary Lasher
HILDAGO JANE	Allison Schubert
LITTLE BECKY TWO-SHOES	Raquel Hecker
MRS. MILLENNIUM	Bellavia Mauro
DR. BILLEAUX	Zachary Lasher
MRS. O'HENRY	Kristen Anderson
CLADWELL'S SECRETARY	Raquel Hecker

| MORE POOR | Victor Khodadad, Terry Cosentino, Rob Maitner |
| UGC EXECUTIVES | Victor Khodadad, Allison Schubert, Nick Balaban |

Opened Off-Broadway at the American Theatre of Actors on May 6, 2001, with the same cast as the Broadway production, except that the roles of Little Becky Two-Shoes and Mrs. Millennium were created and performed by Megan Lawrence.

The following text is based on the production of *Urinetown* that opened at the Henry Miller on Broadway, September 20, 2001. Produced by the Araca Group and Dodger Theatricals in association with TheaterDreams, Inc., and Lauren Mitchell. Directed by John Rando. Musical staging: John Carrafa. Scenic / environment design: Scott Pask; costume design: Gregory Gale and Jonathan Bixby; lighting design: Brian MacDevitt; sound design: Jeff Curtis and Lew Meade; wig / hair design: Darlene Dannenfelser; fight director: Rick Sordelet; orchestrations: Bruce Coughlin; musical direction: Edward Strauss; conductor: Ed Goldschneider; music coordinator: John Miller; production managers: Kai Brothers and Tech Production Services, Inc.; casting: Jay Binder, Laura Stanczyk, and Cindi Rush; production stage manager: Julia P. Jones; general management: Dodger Management Group; marketing: Dodger Marketing; press representatives: Boneau / Bryan-Brown.

CAST OF CHARACTERS IN THE BROADWAY
PRODUCTION (in order of appearance)

OFFICER LOCKSTOCK	Jeff McCarthy
PENELOPE PENNYWISE	Nancy Opel
BOBBY STRONG	Hunter Foster
LITTLE SALLY	Spencer Kayden
HOPE CLADWELL	Jennifer Laura Thompson
MR. MCQUEEN	David Beach
SENATOR FIPP	John Deyle
OLD MAN STRONG / HOT BLADES HARRY	Ken Jennings

SOUPY SUE / CLADWELL'S SECRETARY	Rachel Coloff
TINY TOM / DR. BILLEAUX	Rick Crom
LITTLE BECKY TWO-SHOES / MRS. MILLENNIUM	Jennifer Cody
ROBBY THE STOCKFISH / UGC EXECUTIVE #2	Victor W. Hawks
OFFICER BARREL	Daniel Marcus
BILLY BOY BILL / UGC EXECUTIVE #1	Lawrence E. Street
JOSEPHINE STRONG / OLD WOMAN	Kay Walbye
CALDWELL B. CLADWELL	John Cullum

A Gotham-like city

Sometime after the Stink Years

OFFICER LOCKSTOCK, *a policeman*

LITTLE SALLY, *a poor little girl*

BOBBY STRONG, *assistant custodian at the poorest, filthiest urinal in town*

CALDWELL B. CLADWELL, *president and owner of Urine Good Co.*

HOPE CLADWELL, *Cladwell's daughter; she's new in town*

PENELOPE PENNYWISE, *chief custodian at the poorest, filthiest urinal in town*

OFFICER BARREL, *Lockstock's partner*

MR. MCQUEEN, *Cladwell's right-hand man*

SENATOR FIPP, *a public servant*

OLD MAN STRONG, *a poor man, Bobby's father, also known as Joseph Strong*

JOSEPHINE STRONG, *a poor woman, Bobby's mother, also known as Old Ma Strong*

HOT BLADES HARRY, *a poor man*

SOUPY SUE, *a poor woman*

TINY TOM, *a poor boy*

LITTLE BECKY TWO-SHOES, *a poor woman*

ROBBY THE STOCKFISH, *a poor man*
BILLY BOY BILL, *a poor man*

MRS. MILLENNIUM, *a Urine Good Co. (UGC) executive*
DR. BILLEAUX, *a UGC executive, head of research*
CLADWELL'S SECRETARY, *a valued UGC employee*
UGC EXECUTIVES

COPS—*and lots of them*

ACT I

Scene 1

Early morning. The poorest, filthiest urinal in town. Above the entrance to the urinal hangs a sign that reads Public Amenity #9. THE POOR *lie sprawled across the stage, sleeping quietly. Music for "Urinetown" plays softly in the background.* OFFICER LOCKSTOCK *enters from the house, inspecting the theater for orderliness. Satisfied, he takes his place onstage and addresses the audience directly.*

LOCKSTOCK: Well, hello there. And welcome—to *Urinetown!* (*Pause.*) Not the place, of course. The musical. Urinetown "the place" is . . . well, it's a place you'll hear people referring to a lot throughout the show.

(PENELOPE PENNYWISE *and* BOBBY STRONG *enter. They carry with them a small table upon which rests a ledger.*)

PENNY: You hear the news? They carted Old So-and-So off to Urinetown the other day.

BOBBY: Is that so? What he do?

PENNY: Oh, such-and-such, I hear.

BOBBY: Well, what do you know? Old So-and-So.

(*Bobby and Penny set up their workstation, placing the table beside the entrance to the amenity as* THE POOR *begin to rise.*)

LOCKSTOCK: It's kind of a mythical place, you understand. A bad place. A place you won't see until Act Two. And then . . . ? Well, let's just say it's filled with symbolism and things like that.

(THE POOR *sing the "Urinetown" theme on an "ooh" ever so softly as they prepare for another day.* LITTLE SALLY *enters, counting her pennies.*)

LOCKSTOCK: But *Urinetown* "the musical," well, here we are. Welcome. It takes place in a town like any town . . . that you might find in a musical. This here's the first setting for the show. As the sign says, it's a "public amenity," meaning public toilet. These people have been waiting for hours to get in; it's the only amenity they can afford to get into.

(LITTLE SALLY *approaches* LOCKSTOCK.)

LITTLE SALLY: Say, Officer Lockstock, is this where you tell the audience about the water shortage?

LOCKSTOCK: What's that, Little Sally?

LITTLE SALLY: You know, the water shortage. The hard times. The drought. A shortage so awful that private toilets eventually became unthinkable. A premise so absurd that—

LOCKSTOCK: Whoa there, Little Sally. Not all at once. They'll hear more about the water shortage in the next scene.

LITTLE SALLY: Oh. I guess you don't want to overload them with too much exposition, huh?

LOCKSTOCK: Everything in its time, Little Sally. You're too young to understand it now, but nothing can kill a show like too much exposition.

LITTLE SALLY: How about bad subject matter?

LOCKSTOCK: Well—

LITTLE SALLY: Or a bad title, even? That could kill a show pretty good.

LOCKSTOCK: Well, Little Sally, suffice it to say that in *Urinetown* (the musical) everyone has to use public bathrooms in order to take care of their private business. That's the central conceit of the showww! *(He sings.)*

Better hope your pennies
Add up to the fee—
We can't have you peeing
For free.
If you do, we'll catch you.

We, we never fail!
And we never bother with jail.

(MCQUEEN, FIPP, *and* BARREL *enter. All sing.*)

ALL:
You'll get Urinetown!
Off you'll go to Urinetown!
Away with you to Urinetown!

LOCKSTOCK:
You won't need bail.

(HOPE CLADWELL *enters. As* LOCKSTOCK *and* LITTLE SALLY *speak,* HOPE *approaches* BOBBY *at his table.*)

LOCKSTOCK: Later on you'll learn that these public bathrooms are controlled by a private company. They keep admission high, generally, so if you're down on your luck, you have to come to a place like this—one of the poorest, filthiest urinals in town.

LITTLE SALLY: And you can't just go in the bushes either—there's laws against it.

LOCKSTOCK: That's right, Little Sally. Harsh laws, too. That's why Little Sally here's counting her pennies. Isn't that so, Little Sally?

LITTLE SALLY: I'm very close, Officer. Only a few pennies away.

LOCKSTOCK: Aren't we all, Little Sally. Aren't we all.

(LITTLE SALLY *keeps counting.*)

HOPE: Excuse me, sir, but can you tell me the way to the private company that controls these public bathrooms?

BOBBY: You mean Urine Good Company?

HOPE: That's the one.

LOCKSTOCK: (*To the audience*) You'll meet the guy who runs Urine Good Company later. That there's his daughter.

BOBBY: It's quite a ways from here, ma'am. This here's the bad part of town.

HOPE: So it is.

BOBBY: But if you squint, you can just make out their headquarters rising above the skyline.

HOPE: The gleaming tower on the hill?

BOBBY: That's the one.

HOPE: Gosh, it's beautiful.

BOBBY: You most certainly are.

HOPE: Pardon?

BOBBY: It most certainly is.

HOPE: Oh dear, I'm late already. Thanks ever so much for the directions and such. Bye! *(She exits.)*

BOBBY: Anytime.

LOCKSTOCK: *(To the audience)* Well, we've talked on long enough, I imagine. Enjoy the show. And welcome—to *Urinetown* (the musical)!

(All sing.)

WOMEN:	MEN:
You, our humble audience,	
You have come to see	*You, our humble audience,*
What it's like when	*You have come to see*
People can't pee free.	*People can't pee,*
	People can't pee free,
	Can't pee free.
First act lasts an hour.	
Don't assume you're fine.	*First act lasts an hour.*
Best go now, there often is a line.	*Don't assume you're fine.*
	Often is a,
	Often is a line.

ALL:

This is Urinetown!
One restroom here at Urinetown!
It's unisex at Urinetown!
All by design.

LOCKSTOCK, MCQUEEN, FIPP, BARREL:

It's the oldest story—
Masses are oppressed;
Faces, clothes, and bladders
All distressed.
Rich folks get the good life,
Poor folks get the woe.
In the end, it's nothing you don't know.

ALL:

You're at Urinetown!
Your ticket should say "Urinetown"!
No refunds, this is Urinetown!
We'll keep that dough!

SOPRANOS:	ALTOS:	TENORS:	BASSES:
		This is	
	This is	*Urinetown!*	
People	*Urinetown!*	*Here we are in*	*It's the oldest*
can't pee free!	*Here we are in*	*Urinetown!*	*story!*
People	*Urinetown!*	*This, this is*	*It's the oldest*
can't pee free!	*This is*	*Urinetown!*	*story!*
People	*Urinetown!*	*Here we are in*	*It's the oldest*
can't pee free, they	*Here we are in*	*Urinetown! Yes,*	*story, with*
can't pee free in	*Urinetown,*	*here we are in*	*masses op-*
	yes this is	*Urinetown!*	
Urinetown!	*Urinetown!*	*Urinetown!*	*pressed! Masses,*
		Yes, this is	

Urinetown!	*Urinetown!*	*Urinetown!*	*masses*
		Yes, this is	*oppressed*
			in
Urinetown!	*Urinetown!*	*Urinetown!*	*Urinetown!*

ALL:

On with the show!

*(*LOCKSTOCK, BARREL, MCQUEEN, *and* FIPP *exit as* PENNY *shouts out instructions to* THE POOR.*)*

PENNY: All right, folks, you know the drill. Form a line and have yer money ready. We'll not be repeating yesterday's fiasco, and that means you, Old Man Strong.

*(*THE POOR *crowd around the amenity, forming a line.*)*

LITTLE SALLY: . . . Four hundred and ninety-six. Four hundred and ninety-seven. Just a few more.

*(*MCQUEEN *enters, now on his way to work.* LITTLE SALLY *rushes toward him, her hand stretched out in supplication.*)*

LITTLE SALLY: Penny for a pee, sir?

*(*MCQUEEN *exits.* SENATOR FIPP *enters.*)*

LITTLE SALLY: Please, sir, spare a penny for a morning pee, sir?

FIPP: What's that?

LITTLE SALLY: Or a nickel or a dime?

FIPP: Out of my way, child! I've peeing of my own to tend to.

LITTLE SALLY: But—

*(*FIPP *exits.* LITTLE SALLY *joins the crowd. At the entrance to the amenity* OLD MAN STRONG *is arguing with* PENNY.*)*

OLD MAN STRONG: I haven't got it!

PENNY: Then go get it!

OLD MAN STRONG: C'mon, Penny, I'm good for it.

PENNY: That's what you said last week and I still haven't seen penny one. And it's Ms. Pennywise to you.

OLD MAN STRONG: Bobby! Bobby, reason with the woman. I'm a little short this morning.

TINY TOM: No shorter than yesterday. Unless I've grown.

BOBBY: He's my pa, Ms. Pennywise. Can't he come in for free? Just this once?

PENNY: Get your head out of the clouds, Bobby Strong. No one gets in for free.

OLD MAN STRONG: Now, Ms. Pennywise, we've all had to make special . . . arrangements with people in high places over the years. Why not let this one be ours?

SOUPY SUE: If Old Man Strong gets in for free, then so do I!

TINY TOM: And I!

LITTLE BECKY TWO-SHOES: And I!

PENNY: Quiet back there! No one's gettin' anywhere for free! Don't you think I have bills of my own to pay?! Don't you think I have taxes and tariffs and payoffs to meet, too?! Well, I do! *(Musical vamp for "It's a Privilege to Pee" begins.)* And I don't pay them with promises, see. I pay them with cash! Cold hard cash. Every morning you all come here. And every morning some of you got reasons why ya ain't gonna pay. And I'm here to tell ya, ya is gonna pay!

BOBBY: But, Ms. Penny—

PENNY: No buts, Bobby.

OLD MAN STRONG: In the name of God, Penny, what difference could it make?

PENNY: What difference?!! *(Outraged, she sings.)*
"Times are hard."
"Our cash is tight."
"You've got no right!" I've heard it all before.
"Just this once"
Is once too much,
For once they've onced, they'll want to once once more.

I run the only toilet in this part of town, you see.
So, if you've got to go,
You've got to go through me.

It's a privilege to pee.
Water's worth its weight in gold these days.
No more bathrooms like the olden days.
You come here and pay a fee
For the privilege to pee.

Twenty years we've had the drought,
And our reservoirs have all dried up.
I take my baths now in a coffee cup.
I boil what's left of it for tea,
And it's a privilege to pee.

The politicians in their wisdom saw
That there should be a law.
The politicians taxed the toilets
And made illegal
Public urination and defecation.

So, come and give your coins to me.
Write your name here in the record book.
The authorities will want to look
If you've been regular with me,
If you've paid the proper fee,
For the privilege to pee.
(THE POOR *sing the refrain "It's a privilege to pee" under the following.*)
BOBBY: But, Ms. Pennywise—

PENNY: I said no buts, Bobby. You're a sweet-lookin' boy and I likes to keep you around, but this man ain't comin' in without payin'. Not this time.

OLD MAN STRONG: I can't wait much longer, Bobby. There's no tellin' what I might do!

PENNY:
You think you've got some kind of right?

THE POOR:
Kind of right, kind of right!

PENNY:
You think you'll come in here and go for free?

THE POOR:
Snag a freebie!

PENNY:
The only thing you'll get is "no" for free!

THE POOR:
Negatory!

PENNY:
I'm a business gal, you see.

THE POOR:
Business gal, you see!

PENNY:	**THE POOR:**
I sell the privilege to pee!	*It's a privilege to pee!*

PENNY:
The good Lord made us so we'd piss each day
Until we piss away.
The good Lord made sure that what goes in men
Must soon come out again,
So you're no different, then,
From lowly me.

THE POOR:
Me,
Lowly me,
Lowly me,

Lowly me,
Lowly me!

BOBBY: But, Ms. Pennywise—

OLD MAN STRONG: That's enough, Bobby.

PENNY:
And I think I'll charge you twice,

OLD MAN STRONG:
No need to jeopardize your position.

PENNY:
Or better yet, have you arrested

OLD MAN STRONG: I'm through with all this, you see.

PENNY:
Since you prefer the law gets tested.

OLD MAN STRONG: Scrapin' cash three times a day.

PENNY:
And in Urinetown you'll see

OLD MAN STRONG: Crazy with the nitrates half the time.

PENNY:
Why it's dumb to fight with me

OLD MAN STRONG: It's no way to live, I tells ya! No way to live!

PENNY:
For the privilege to pee!

POOR:
Wah! Wah!

PENNY AND POOR:
Wah!

(OLD MAN STRONG *finds a wall and undoes his pants to pee.*)

BOBBY: Pa! Pa, what are ya doin'?! Have ya lost your mind?!

OLD MAN STRONG: More than that, boy! A whole lot more than that! *(He starts peeing. A police whistle is heard in the distance.)*

SOUPY SUE: Looky there!

ROBBY THE STOCKFISH: It's Old Man Strong! He ain't waitin'!

LITTLE BECKY TWO-SHOES: He's peein' right there on the pavement, he is!

TINY TOM: If he's goin', then I'm goin'!

(OFFICERS LOCKSTOCK and BARREL enter.)

LOCKSTOCK: Oh no, you're not!

BARREL: All right, then! Make way!

LOCKSTOCK: Make way, damn you! Make way!

OLD MAN STRONG: Ahhh. That's better.

BARREL: So, if it ain't Old Man Strong.

OLD MAN STRONG: The same.

LOCKSTOCK: Is this your doing, Strong?

OLD MAN STRONG: It is.

LOCKSTOCK: Seize him!

(BARREL seizes OLD MAN STRONG.)

THE POOR: *[Gasp.]*

LOCKSTOCK: You've done a terrible thing here today, Strong.

OLD MAN STRONG: I did what I thought was necessary.

PENNY: Grab a mop, Bobby. Never thought I'd live to see the day.

LOCKSTOCK: Breaking the Public Health Act is an exiling offense, Strong.

BARREL: Quite exiling.

OLD MAN STRONG: What if it is? I feel better now, and that's all I cares about.

BOBBY: Oh, Pa.

LOCKSTOCK: Always knew we'd get you in the end, Joseph Strong. Take him away!

(BARREL drags OLD MAN STRONG away.)

OLD MAN STRONG: Bobby!

BOBBY: Pa!

OLD MAN STRONG: Don't forget me, Bobby!

BOBBY: I won't, Pa!

OLD MAN STRONG: And tell yer mother . . . tell yer mother that I love her!

BOBBY: I will, Pa! I will!

OLD MAN STRONG: Remember me, boys! Oh God, what have I done?! Remember me!

(They exit. LOCKSTOCK *sings.)*

LOCKSTOCK:
Remember, Bobby, what became of him.

THE POOR:
Remember!

LOCKSTOCK:
How he indulged a whim.

THE POOR:
Remember!

LOCKSTOCK:
Remember how he made a mockery.
He shunned the crockery.
Off to the dockery!
Don't be like him.

*(*THE POOR *sing the refrain "Don't be like him" under the following.)*

BOBBY: "What became of him"? What do you mean by that?

LOCKSTOCK: Just keep your head out of the clouds, that's all I'm saying. Good day. *(He exits.)*

PENNY: All right, who's ready to pay?!

SOUPY SUE: It's my last few dollars, but I'll pay.

TINY TOM: Me, too!

LITTLE BECKY TWO-SHOES: Me, too!

SOUPY SUE: We'll all pay, Bobby Strong! Always and forever, just so long as you keep lettin' us pay!

BOBBY: Oh, Pa! What's to become of you?

PENNY: Back to work, then, Bobby! The morning rush is on!

Scene 2

The executive offices of Urine Good Company. CALDWELL B. CLAD-
WELL, *with* MR. MCQUEEN *at his side, is meeting with* SENATOR FIPP.

FIPP: Where's my dough?!

CLADWELL: Isn't that what we're all asking ourselves, Senator?
Where's my dough? From the cop walking his beat to the little
baby asleep in his mother's arms, we're all asking the same
question: Where's my dough? And by dough, of course, I
mean money.

FIPP: I made my speech! Where's my dough?!

CLADWELL: Oh, there'll be plenty of dough for everyone, Senator, once the new fee hikes breeze through the Legislature.

FIPP: I was hoping to wait for the vote during my latest fact-
finding mission—to Rio! Wouldn't want to be around once
the new fee hikes breeze through.

CLADWELL: You think I've gone too far this time, don't you, Fipp?

(HOPE enters.)

FIPP: It's a powder keg out there, Cladwell. This time I think it's
gonna blow!

HOPE: Daddy?

CLADWELL, FIPP, AND MCQUEEN: Whaa—?!

CLADWELL: Hope darling, I thought you'd never get here!

(They embrace.)

HOPE: Sorry I'm late, Daddy. I left just as soon as my exams were
finished.

CLADWELL: How's everything, dear?

HOPE: Fine, Daddy. Just fine. It feels great to be done with
school. Finally.

CLADWELL: You see there, Mister McQueen! Beautiful, big-
hearted, and now with a head filled with the best stuff money
can buy.

MCQUEEN: Well, if the stuff in her head is nearly as big as the stuff in her heart, I'm sure she'll be running this company in no time. *(MCQUEEN laughs. CLADWELL doesn't.)*

CLADWELL: That'll be all, Mister McQueen.

MCQUEEN: Yes, of course.

(He exits. FIPP approaches HOPE.)

FIPP: Well, I'll be. Hope Cladwell, and all grown up, too.

HOPE: Hello, Senator.

FIPP: Come to join your father's little operation?

HOPE: It's just a fax/copy position, of course. First day.

FIPP: A fax/copy girl, huh? *(Taking her hand)* Well, your father mentioned he was bringing on a new fax /copy girl. He neglected, however, to mention how beautiful she'd be. You'd be. You're so beautiful. Even as a little girl I always thought—

CLADWELL: That's enough, Fipp.

FIPP: Yes, of course.

CLADWELL: Well, we won't keep you, Senator; it's a big day. I'm sure you'll have your hands full on the floor of the Legislature, what with the fee-hike vote and all.

FIPP: Oh, they'll be full, Cladwell. And by this time tomorrow I fully expect them to be full of cash.

CLADWELL: Oh, they'll be full of cash, Senator. We'll all be full of cash, provided the vote comes through.

FIPP: Oh, the vote will come through, Cladwell. It'll come through just as long as you come through with the cash.

CLADWELL: No worries there, Senator. Once the vote comes through, there'll be nothing else to come through but the cash.

FIPP: And no need to worry about the vote—

CLADWELL: Fipp! I think we understand each other.

FIPP: Yes. Well. Goodbye. *(He exits.)*

CLADWELL: Let's meet the staff. Staff!

(UGC STAFF enters.)

CLADWELL: Staff, this here's my daughter—and our newest fax/copy girl—Hope Cladwell. Hope Cladwell, the good people of Urine Good Company, or UGC, as it's known for short.

HOPE: Hello, everybody!

UGC STAFF: Hello, Hope!

CLADWELL: Say a few words, Hope darling.

HOPE: Well . . . uh . . . it's a great company and I hope to help you make it even greater.

(All applaud.)

CLADWELL: Well, that's absolutely right, Hope dear, absolutely right. For you see, ladies and gentlemen, twenty years ago we came to the people of this community with a simple proposition: Look the other way while we run this company the way we see fit, and we will keep the pee off the street and the water in the ground. Hope here has come to join our little operation, to help us keep that promise, so promise me you'll treat her like the Cladwell she is, for one day (*Vamp for "Mister Cladwell" begins.*) she may be standing in the shoes you see me wearing today, the shoes I wore when I made that promise those many years ago. *(He sings.)*

I saw gray skies, foreboding and cold!
I saw gray skies and made them rain gold!
Now those skies aren't so bleak to behold!
They're still gray,
But they pay
For your sal'ries tenfold!

I took this town that formerly stank,
I took this town and made it smell swank!
I made flushing mean flush at the bank!
I'm the man

With the plan,
And so whom should you thank?

MCQUEEN:

Whom?

CHORUS:

Mister Cladwell,
We're so thankful
For that bank full of dough!
You're a toreador,
And it's cash that you gore!
Could we hope for much more?
We really doubt it!

CLADWELL:

You may be right there!

CHORUS:

Mister Cladwell,
You've got riches,
Which is just what we need!

We say
Hail to you, the duke of the ducats!

CLADWELL:

I can bring in bucks by the buckets!

CHORUS:

You're the master, you're making money!

CLADWELL:

Faster still than bees making honey!

CHORUS:

You're Mister Cladwell!

HOPE: Gosh, I never realized large, monopolizing corporations could be such a force for good in the world.

CLADWELL: Few do.

TOP LEFT: Greg Kotis (top) and Ayun Halliday, Paris, 1995 (GREG KOTIS)

TOP RIGHT: The Cardiff Giant Theater Company ensemble, Chicago, 1988. Clockwise from left: Greg Kotis, Mark Hollmann, John Hildreth, Bob Fisher, and Phil Ridarelli (CAROLYN SCHNEIDER/MS. SCHNEIDER IS SOLE OWNER OF IMAGE)

BOTTOM: The New York company of the Neo-Futurists, 1995. From left to right: Bill Coelius, Greg Kotis, Ayun Halliday, Spencer Kayden, and Robert Neill (PHOTOGRAPH BY ROBERT C. COELIUS)

TOP: The cast of the 1999 New York International Fringe Festival production of *Urinetown*. Clockwise from upper left: Kristen Anderson, Nick Balaban, Wilson Hall, Louise Rozett, Victor Khodadad, Zachary Lasher, Terry Cosentino, Jay Rhoderick, Rob Maitner, Adam Grant, Allison Schubert, Carol Hickey, Bellavia Mauro, Spencer Kayden, and Raquel Hecker (GREG KOTIS)

BOTTOM: Director John Rando with the scale model of Scott Pask's scenic/environment design for the off-Broadway production of *Urinetown*, New York City, 2001 (GREG KOTIS)

TOP LEFT: From the Fringe to the Great White Way: Spencer Kayden as Little Sally with Jay Rhoderick as Officer Lockstock in the 1999 New York International Fringe Festival production

(DANNY SHAPIRO/FROM THE SHAPIRO ARCHIVES)

TOP RIGHT: Spencer on Broadway with Jeff McCarthy as Officer Lockstock (© 2001, JOAN MARCUS)

BOTTOM: The final tableau from "Urinetown," the opening number of *Urinetown*, as performed in the off-Broadway production at the American Theatre of Actors, New York City, 2001. Top row, on catwalk, from left to right: David Beach, John Deyle, and Daniel Marcus. Middle row, standing, from left to right: Kay Walbye, Spencer Kayden, Rachel Coloff, Nancy Opel, and Hunter Foster. Front row, kneeling, from left to right: Rick Crom, Ken Jennings, Jeff McCarthy, Lawrence E. Street, and Victor W. Hawks (© 2001, JOAN MARCUS)

RIGHT: Nancy Opel as Penelope Pennywise sings "It's a Privilege to Pee" (© 2001, JOAN MARCUS)

BELOW: The corporate minions of Urine Good Company idolize their leader, "Mr. Cladwell," in the off-Broadway production. From left to right: Lawrence E. Street, Victor W. Hawks, John Cullum, Rachel Coloff, and Megan Lawrence (© 2001, JOAN MARCUS)

LEFT: Jennifer Laura Thompson as Hope advises Hunter Foster as Bobby to "Follow Your Heart"

(© 2001, JOAN MARCUS))

BOTTOM: Hope (Jennifer Laura Thompson) asks her father, Caldwell B. Cladwell (John Cullum), if he believes in love

(© 2001, JOAN MARCUS)

TOP: John Deyle as Senator Fipp, John Cullum as Caldwell B. Cladwell, and David Beach as Mr. McQueen oversee the quashing of Bobby's revolution in the Act One Finale (© 2001, JOAN MARCUS)

BOTTOM: The Poor, backing up Bobby Strong, their revolutionary leader, sing "Free, people are free!" in the Act One Finale of *Urinetown* as performed on Broadway at the Henry Miller Theatre, 2001. From left to right: Victor W. Hawks, Kay Walbye, Lawrence E. Street, Jennifer Cody, Hunter Foster, Rachel Coloff, Ken Jennings, Rick Crom (hidden behind Jennings), and Spencer Kayden

(© 2001, JOAN MARCUS)

TOP: The Poor conspire to "Snuff that Girl" in the off-Broadway production. Clockwise from left: Rick Crom, Rachel Coloff, Megan Lawrence, Lawrence E. Street, Ken Jennings, Victor W. Hawks, Spencer Kayden, and (seated) Jennifer Laura Thompson

LEFT: Jeff McCarthy and Daniel Marcus as Officers Lockstock and Barrel prepare to send Hunter Foster as Bobby Strong to Urinetown in "Why Did I Listen to that Man?"

Hope tells Cladwell that she intends to send him to Urinetown. From left to right: Victor W. Hawks, Lawrence E. Street, John Cullum, Rachel Coloff, and Jennifer Laura Thompson (© 2001, JOAN MARCUS)

MCQUEEN:

All those coins that we take from the throng
End up here where those coins all belong.
Lots of coins make our company strong!

CLADWELL:

Charging fees
As we please
Is our right—it's not wrong!

MCQUEEN:

We're not greedy, as some make us seem.
We need funds for our big research team.

DR. BILLEAUX:

Men in labcoats and test tubes with steam!

CLADWELL AND MCQUEEN:

What it shows
No one knows,
But, hey, still we can dream!

MCQUEEN:

Of!

CHORUS:

Mister Cladwell,
Finding answers,
Curing cancers of doubt!

Your ambitions are high,
But you're humble as pie!
What a wonderful guy!
We simply love you!

HOPE:

Da—
Da, da, da, da, Daddy!

That's my dad!

CLADWELL:

You're making me blush now!

CHORUS:
Doodle-oodle-ooo!
Doodle-oodle-ooo!
Doodle-oodle-
Oodle-oodle-
Oodle-oodle-
Oodle-oodle!

WOMEN:	**MEN:**
Boom!	
	Boom!
Boom!	
	Boom!

CHORUS:
Boom!
Mister Cladwell,
You're so godly,
Oddly perfect and right!

MEN:
You are continental, yet unpretentious!

WOMEN:
Fancy-free, yet so conscientious!

MEN:
Wise but trendy, tough as a mountain!

CHORUS:
Goodness flows from you like a fountain!
You're Mister, you're Mister

CLADWELL:
Cladwell!

CHORUS:
Cladwell!

HOPE: Gosh, Daddy, they certainly do seem to adore you. So why do I feel so conflicted?

CLADWELL: Nonsense. Did I send you to the Most Expensive University in the World to teach you how to feel conflicted, or to learn how to manipulate great masses of people?

HOPE: To learn how to manipulate great masses of people, Daddy.

CLADWELL: Which is exactly what we'll do. Now get faxing!

HOPE: And copying!

CLADWELL: And—welcome home.

Scene 3

Night. A street corner. LITTLE SALLY *counts her pennies.* OFFICER LOCKSTOCK *enters.*

LITTLE SALLY: . . . Five hundred and thirty-seven, five hundred and thirty-eight, just a few more . . .

LOCKSTOCK: Well, hello there, Little Sally. Awfully late for a little girl to be out and about. Especially on a night like tonight.

LITTLE SALLY: Oh. Just tryin' to scrape together a few coins before the late-night rush is all. Got one to spare?

LOCKSTOCK: Sure, Little Sally. I'm in a good mood tonight. *(He tosses her a coin.)*

LITTLE SALLY: Gee, thanks. *(She squirrels the coin away.)* Say, Officer Lockstock, I was thinkin'. We don't spend much time on hydraulics, do we?

LOCKSTOCK: Hydraulics, Little Sally?

LITTLE SALLY: You know, hydraulics. Hydration. Irrigation. Or just plain old laundry. Seems to me that with all the talk of water shortage and drought and whatnot, we might spend some time on those things, too. After all, a dry spell would affect hydraulics, too, you know.

LOCKSTOCK: Why, sure it would, Little Sally. But . . . How shall I put it? Sometimes—in a musical—it's better to focus on one big thing rather than a lot of little things. The audience tends to be much happier that way. And it's easier to write.

(LITTLE SALLY *thinks this over.*)

LITTLE SALLY: One big thing, huh?

LOCKSTOCK: That's right, Little Sally.

LITTLE SALLY: Oh. *(Pause.)* Then why not hydraulics?

LOCKSTOCK: *(Chuckles.)* Run along, then, Little Sally. Wouldn't want you to miss last call. Ms. Pennywise won't hold the gate forever, you know.

LITTLE SALLY: Oh, yeah, right. Thanks for the coin! Bye!

(She hurries off. BARREL *enters, carrying a shovel and a mop.*)

BARREL: What a night.

LOCKSTOCK: Everything cleaned up all right, Mister Barrel?

BARREL: Sure, same as always. Did you hear him scream, though, Mister Lockstock?

LOCKSTOCK: Old Man Strong?

BARREL: All the way down to Urinetown.

LOCKSTOCK: Oh yes, I heard him, Mister Barrel. But then, they all seem to scream in the end, now, don't they? As their long journey into "exile" comes to a close and the spires of Urinetown peek above the horizon? They do scream then, Mister Barrel. They most certainly do.

(They laugh.)

BARREL: I suppose I thought he might be different, somehow.

LOCKSTOCK: Different?

BARREL: Old Man Strong. Always seemed a bit tougher than the rest. I was hoping he might . . . I don't know . . . surprise us, somehow.

(Vamp begins for "Cop Song.")

LOCKSTOCK: If there's one thing I've learned in my years enforcing the laws of this city, it's that the journey down to Urinetown offers no surprises. Not even from the very toughest amongst us. On that journey expect only the expected. *(He sings.)*

It's a hard, cold tumble of a journey,
Worthy of a gurney, a bumble down,
A slapped face, smacked with a mace,
Certain to debase, is our stumble down.

It's a path that leads you only one place,
Horrible to retrace, a crumble down.
A hard, cold tumble of a tourney,
Jumble of a journey to Urinetown.

LOCKSTOCK AND BARREL:
Julie Cassidy
Went to a field behind a tree,
Saw there was no one who could see

LOCKSTOCK:
Her pee

BARREL:
But me!

LOCKSTOCK AND BARREL:
And Jacob Rosenbloom
Thought he was safe up in his room,
Didn't know the jars he kept up there
Would obligate a trip to a urine tomb!
(More COPS *enter.)*

LOCKSTOCK:
There are those who think our methods vicious—

BARREL:
Overly malicious—

LOCKSTOCK:

A bunch of brutes. But it's we who gather for the people—

BARREL:

Tavern to the steeple—

LOCKSTOCK AND BARREL:

Lawful fruits!

LOCKSTOCK:

Our task: bring a little order—

BARREL:

Swindle out a hoarder—

LOCKSTOCK:

From what he loots. As the book says, "Certainly a season"—

BARREL:

Trample out a treason—

ALL:

With hobnail boots!
Roger Roosevelt
Kept a cup below his belt,
Cup ran over when he knelt.

LOCKSTOCK:

He smelt—

BARREL:

We dealt.

ALL:

And Joseph "Old Man" Strong
Held his pee for much too long,
Hoped his son might bail him out.
His guess was good but also wrong!

LOCKSTOCK:

Years past all lived in a jungle,
Scooping out a bungle, nature's bowl.
Life of constant deprivation,
Certain aggravation took its toll.

Soon learned power of the truncheon.
Organize a function, king to pawn.
So if peace is what you're after,
Urinetown's the rafter to hang it on.

GIRL COP 1:
Julie Cassidy—

BOY COP 1:	**BOY COP 2:**
Jacob Rosenbloom—	
	Roger
Jacob Rosenbloom—	*Roosevelt—*

LOCKSTOCK AND BARREL:	**BOY COP 3:**	**GIRL COP 1:**
		Julie
	Joseph	*Cassidy—*
Don't be like them!	*Old Man Strong—*	

LOCKSTOCK AND BARREL:	**GIRL COPS:**	**BOY COPS:**
Don't be like them!	*Don't be like them!*	
Don't be like them!	*Don't be like them!*	*Don't be like them!*
Don't be like them!	*Don't be like them!*	*Don't be like them!*

LOCKSTOCK AND BARREL:	**GIRL COPS:**	**BOY COPS:**
It's a hard, cold		
Tumble of a journey,	*It's a hard, cold*	
Worthy of a gurney,	*Tumble of a journey,*	*It's a hard, cold*
A bumble down,	*Worthy of a gurney,*	*Tumble of a journey,*
A slapped face,	*A bumble down,*	*Worthy of a gurney,*
Smacked with a mace,	*A slapped face,*	*A bumble down,*
Certain to debase,	*Smacked with a mace,*	*A slapped face,*
Is our stumble down.	*Certain to debase.*	*Smacked with a*
		mace.

ALL:

It's a path that leads you only one place,
Horrible to retrace, a crumble down,
A hard, cold tumble of a tourney,
Jumble of a journey to Urinetown!

LOCKSTOCK: Off you go, then, boys. And happy hunting.

(The COPS *scramble off.* LOCKSTOCK *and* BARREL *linger.)*

BARREL: Hm . . . yes. So, have you made plans for your journey yet?

LOCKSTOCK: To Urinetown?!

BARREL: To Rio, of course.

LOCKSTOCK: Oh. Yes. Rio. Well, I had to squeeze Cladwell a bit tighter than usual for our monthly payoffs, extortion fees, money bribes, and such. But—

(HOPE enters.)

BARREL: Caution, Mister Lockstock. It would seem we're no longer alone.

LOCKSTOCK: Well, I'll be.

BARREL: If I'm not mistaken, that there's his daughter.

LOCKSTOCK: So it is. And all grown up, too. *(To* HOPE*)* Ms. Cladwell! A little late for you to be out, don't you think?

HOPE: Oh, hello, Officers.

LOCKSTOCK: If I didn't know better, I'd say you were on a late-night-behind-the-bushes-to-relieve-yourself-for-free kind of walk.

HOPE: Oh no, Officers. I'm just coming home from work. First day.

BARREL: Long hours.

LOCKSTOCK: Just like us.

HOPE: There's some kind of big vote down at the Legislature tonight. Plenty of faxing to do.

BARREL: And copying, I imagine.

HOPE: Oh yes. And copying.

(LOCKSTOCK takes HOPE's hand.)

LOCKSTOCK: I must say, Ms. Cladwell, your father mentioned the size and purity of your heart. He neglected, however, to mention the size and purity of your beauty. *(He kisses her hand.)*

HOPE: Does beauty have a size, Officer?

LOCKSTOCK: In some countries.

(BOBBY STRONG enters, unseen.)

LOCKSTOCK: I'd take care on these streets late at night, Ms. Cladwell. There's no telling what some people wouldn't do for a few coins.

BARREL: Especially these days, what with the new fee hikes and all.

HOPE: Oh, I'm not afraid of people, Officers.

LOCKSTOCK: Oh, no?

HOPE: Not really. Everyone has a heart, you see. As long as you know that you need never fear a soul.

LOCKSTOCK: Everyone?

HOPE: Everyone.

BARREL: Even criminals?

HOPE: Even criminals.

BOBBY: Even policemen?

LOCKSTOCK AND BARREL: Whaa—?!

BARREL: Bobby Strong!

LOCKSTOCK: Out a bit late, don't you think?

BOBBY: Out late taking care of another late-night rush is all. There's talk of more fee hikes, people are getting edgy.

LOCKSTOCK: Are they? Well, I'm glad to hear you were otherwise engaged. Wouldn't want to put you under suspicion for taking a late-night-behind-the-bushes—

BOBBY: I don't need to do that anymore, Officers. Not while I work for Penny, I don't.

BARREL: But you still need to keep your head out of the clouds now, don't you?

BOBBY: What do you mean by that?

LOCKSTOCK: What he means is, you're a good boy, Bobby Strong. See that you don't end up like your father.

BOBBY: And how did my father end up?

(Pause.)

LOCKSTOCK: Well, we're off. Our work's never done. Good night.

HOPE: Good night, Officers.

BARREL: Good night, Bobby.

(They exit.)

HOPE: You were rather brave with them.

BOBBY: I don't care for policemen. Not those two, anyway.

HOPE: Policemen protect the peace.

BOBBY: Do they?

HOPE: Usually.

(Pause.)

BOBBY: Didn't I see you down by the amenity this morning?

HOPE: That was me. I was rushing off to work, first day.

BOBBY: Find your way all right?

HOPE: The gleaming tower on the hill? Couldn't miss it.

BOBBY: Beautiful.

HOPE: It's rather shiny, that's true enough.

(Pause.)

BOBBY: Did you mean what you said to those policemen? About everyone having a heart?

HOPE: Well, sure I did.

BOBBY: Because . . . well, because mine feels awful cold just now.

HOPE: Cold?

BOBBY: Or empty. One of the two.

HOPE: Not because of me, I hope?

BOBBY: Oh no. Because of something I did.

(The ghost of OLD MAN STRONG *and* TINY TOM *appear in the distance.)*

OLD MAN STRONG: Bobby! Bobby, reason with the woman! I'm a little short this morning!

TINY TOM: No shorter than yesterday. Unless I've grown.

(They disappear.)

BOBBY: Or, rather, something I didn't do.

HOPE: If it feels cold, then it must still be there, don't you think?

BOBBY: Unless there's a vacuum where it used to be.

HOPE: A vacuum? In your chest? It sounds so implausible.

BOBBY: I did something wrong this morning is all I'm trying to say. I can't seem to get it out of my head.

HOPE: The vacuum?

BOBBY: My action. I let someone down that I love dearly. I feel real bad about it.

HOPE: Well, maybe that's nature's way of telling you that now's the time to lift someone up?

BOBBY: Really?

HOPE: Sure. Do you think you'd be feeling as bad as you do if you didn't have a heart?

(Musical vamp begins for "Follow Your Heart.")

BOBBY: I don't know. I suppose not.

HOPE: Of course you wouldn't. Because then you'd be dead. *(She sings.)*

When darkness surrounds you
And you lose your way,
You have your own compass
That turns night to day,
And it's even with you
Before you depart.
Be still, hear it beating,
It's leading you.
Follow your heart.

BOBBY: Follow my heart? But to where?

HOPE: To wherever your heart tells you to go.

BOBBY: Even . . . *(He looks around.)* . . . there?

HOPE: Even to the clouds, if that's what your heart commands. What's it saying now?

BOBBY: I don't know. I don't know how to listen to my heart. *(Music fades.)*

HOPE: You have to listen carefully. Here, let me try. *(She puts her ear to* BOBBY'*s chest.)*

BOBBY: Do you—

HOPE: Sshh! *(Music begins again.)* Ah, there it is. It's saying *(She sings.)*

We all want a world
Filled with peace and with joy,
With plenty of water for each girl and boy.
That bright, shining world
Is just waiting to start.
No meanness or sorrow,
Just cleanness tomorrow,
If only you follow your heart.

You see there? Even your heart knows you should follow your heart.

BOBBY: "Peace and joy." "Plenty of water." I guess I do want those things.

HOPE: There's something else your heart was saying. Maybe something I shouldn't have heard.

BOBBY: There was?

HOPE: I think so. It was barely audible, but I definitely heard something.

BOBBY: Well? What was it?

HOPE: Let me try again, maybe I can make it out this time. *(She listens. Music begins again.)* There it is. So faint . . . it's saying *(She sings.)*

Follow, into the open air,
Far from squalor and noise.

Follow, someone is waiting there,
Someone who shares all your hopes
And your joys.

"Someone is waiting there"? Why, my heart was saying those exact words just the other day.

BOBBY: It was?

HOPE: Sure it was. "Squalor and noise," "hopes and joys." It was telling me about all those things.

BOBBY: I didn't know two hearts could speak as one.

HOPE: I didn't either. Until now. Here, listen.

(She brings BOBBY'*s ear to her chest. He sings.)*

BOBBY:
Someday I'll meet someone
Whose heart joins with mine,
Aortas and arteries all intertwined.
They'll beat so much stronger
Than they could apart.
Eight chambers of muscle to hustle
The love in our heart.

BOBBY AND HOPE:
Love is kind and considerate,
Love is peaceful and fair.
Love can creep up so suddenly—
When you least think of it,
Your love is there.

We all want a world
Filled with peace and with joy,
With plenty of justice
For each girl and boy.
That bright, shining world
Is just waiting to start.

No anger or badness,
Just laughter and gladness,
If only I follow your heart.
(HOPE *extends her hand.*)

HOPE: Well, good night . . .

(BOBBY *takes it.*)

BOBBY: Bobby. Bobby Strong. (*He pulls her close to him.*)

HOPE: Good night, Bobby Strong.

(*They kiss.*)

BOBBY: And good night . . .

HOPE: Hope.

BOBBY: Good night, Hope. I won't forget what you said, about the clouds and my heart.

HOPE: And I won't forget what you said, about the laughter and the gladness.

(*He turns to go.* LOCKSTOCK *and* LITTLE SALLY *enter, unseen.*)

HOPE: Wait a minute, when can I see you again?

BOBBY: In this darkness I'm afraid you can't see me at all. But a bright, shining world is waiting to start, I can feel it. Come to Amenity Number Nine tomorrow. I'll show it to you. (*He exits.*)

LITTLE SALLY: She loves him, doesn't she, Officer Lockstock?

LOCKSTOCK: Sure, she does, Little Sally. He's the hero of the show, she has to love him.

(HOPE *exits.*)

LITTLE SALLY: Yeah. Everyone loves Bobby Strong. (*Pause.*) What's it like, Officer Lockstock?

LOCKSTOCK: What's what like, Little Sally?

LITTLE SALLY: Urinetown.

LOCKSTOCK: Oh, I can't tell you that, Little Sally.

LITTLE SALLY: Why not?

LOCKSTOCK: Because it's a secret, that's why. Its power depends on mystery. I can't just blurt it out, like "There is no Urinetown! We just kill people!" Oh no. The information must be oozed out slowly, until it bursts forth in one mighty, cathartic moment! Somewhere in Act Two. With everybody singing, and things like that.

(Pause.)

LITTLE SALLY: Oh. I get it.

(Scene-change music.)

LOCKSTOCK: Well, I should be going. It's time for the next scene.

LITTLE SALLY: The next morning at the amenity, when the new fee hikes are announced?

LOCKSTOCK: That's the one. So long for now, Little Sally. And keep your head down.

(He exits. Segue into . . .)

Scene 4

The poorest, filthiest urinal in town. BOBBY *enters as* MCQUEEN *concludes an announcement he is delivering to* THE POOR.

MCQUEEN: And so with this piece of paper the UGC awards Amenity Number Nine the first of our new and entirely legal fee hikes, which we hope you all will honor and enjoy.

THE POOR: Enjoy?!/Legal?!/Etc.

MCQUEEN: Of course, no one knows better than the good people at Urine Good Company how difficult times are, but research into finding the long-term solutions we need is expensive. So, for the time being, our decision is firm and we look forward to going to Rio with our new profits. *(Pause.)* I mean, we look forward to finding lasting solutions . . . and things like that. Good luck, Ms. Pennywise, see you in . . . well, you know where. *(He exits.)*

TINY TOM: You can't do this to us, Ms. Pennywise! It'll be off to Urinetown for the lot of us sooner or later if you do!

PENNY: And it'll be off to Urinetown for me if I don't. Now get in line and have your money ready—the new fee-hike money, that is!

BOBBY: Ms. Pennywise!

PENNY: Bobby Strong! Where the hell have you been?!

BOBBY: Sorry I'm late, Ms. Pennywise. I was up all night thinking, is all.

PENNY: Up all night thinking, is it?! You work here now, Bobby, you don't need to go in the bushes anymore.

BOBBY: I wasn't—

PENNY: Like father, like son, that's what I say. Now let's get to work.

BOBBY: But it was about my father that I was thinking, Ms. Pennywise. About what happened to him yesterday. About what's happening to all of us.

PENNY: He broke the law yesterday, Bobby, and that's the end of it.

BOBBY: But what if the law is wrong?

(Pause.)

PENNY: What did you say?

BOBBY: I said, what if the law is wrong, Ms. Pennywise?! What if all this is wrong?!

PENNY: Wrong?! You've got a sweet-lookin' head, Bobby, a sweet-lookin' head! *(Vamp begins for "Look at the Sky.")* But you keep it up there in the clouds day after day after day, and it's gotta come down from there. You hear me?! Get that head out of the clouds, Bobby Strong! You get it out of the clouds!

(She returns to address THE POOR. BOBBY *sings.)*

BOBBY:

Off in the distance there's a beautiful horizon—

PENNY: All right, folks, you know the drill.

BOBBY:

Gleaming and radiant, it's what I'll keep my eyes on—

PENNY: The same as it's always been.

BOBBY:

As the world turns to face the sun and start another day,
It suddenly
Occurs to me
That maybe we can find another way.
Look at the sky,
Full of hope and promise.
It's a shining ideal.
How I reel
When I look at the sky.

PENNY: Now, who's first?

JOSEPHINE STRONG: I am!

BOBBY: Ma!

PENNY: We'll take your fee now, Mrs. Strong. The improved fee,
that is.

BOBBY:

Daily we make them pay their nickels, dimes, and quarters—

JOSEPHINE: But this is all I have, Ms. Pennywise.

BOBBY:

Daily we break them 'cause we have to follow orders.

LITTLE SALLY: Haven't you enough, Mrs. Strong?

BOBBY:

And we keep filling moneybags with broken lives and dreams,
But what's it for?
I can't ignore
These black, immoral profit-making schemes.

Look at the sky,
High above this madness.
Here below, feel our shame.
It must stop in the name
Of the sky.

JOSEPHINE: Here's all I have, Bobby. Is it enough?

BOBBY: You hold on to that money, Ma.

JOSEPHINE: Really?

PENNY: The fee is the law, Bobby Strong. She'll abide by it or she'll join her husband.

BOBBY: And what if there was a new law in town, Ms. Pennywise? A new law that didn't come from any voting process or elected body or process of judicial review, but a brand-new law that came from an organ. That's right, a muscular, blood-pumping organ. *(He thumps his chest.)* Like this one. Right here.

PENNY: A muscular organ?

BOBBY: Can't you see it, Ms. Pennywise? Well, if this one's too small for you, why not try this one on for size?! *(He directs her to look at the sky.)*

PENNY: It's . . . it's blinding me!

BOBBY:
Look at the sky!
There's a great, big heart there!
There's a heart
In the sky.
There just is.
Don't ask why—
It's the sky!

PENNY: Don't do this, Bobby. You'll regret it.

BOBBY: I don't think so. C'mon, Ma. This one's on the house. For everyone! Forever!

THE POOR: Hooray!

SOUPY SUE:
Your heart knows all things great and true—

TINY TOM:
The things mere brains can never know!

JOSEPHINE:
Your heart points to the great, big blue—

THE POOR:
Where the people's allegiance must go!
BOBBY: Tell me where!

THE POOR: **BOBBY:**
Look at the sky!

                                            Look at the sky!

That's our inspiration!

                                            Look at the sky!

THE POOR:
We can win
If we try.
We begin
When we look at the sky!
PENNY: Oh, Bobby, what's to become of you? What's to become
   of us all?! *(She exits.)*

THE POOR: **BOBBY:**
Look at the sky,

                                            Off in the distance
Standard of the people.   *There's a beautiful horizon.*

THE POOR:
It's a banner so wide,
Flying proudly with pride
In the sky—
BOBBY:
In the sky—
THE POOR:
In the sky!

Scene 5

The good offices of Urine Good Company. CLADWELL *confers with* FIPP.

CLADWELL: You'll be off to Rio, then, I imagine?

FIPP: Already got my ticket.

CLADWELL: Good work on the floor of the Legislature, Fipp. It was touch-and-go there for a while, I understand.

FIPP: Well, your "Beaches of Rio" slide show changed their minds soon enough. Just like it changed my mind those many years ago. God, I wish I'd never met you, Caldwell B. Cladwell.

(HOPE enters carrying a stack of papers.)

HOPE: Sorry to interrupt, Daddy. I just wanted to make sure you got your morning faxes.

CLADWELL: Why, Hope, you're absolutely glowing!

FIPP: It would seem that office work agrees with her. What with the faxing and all.

CLADWELL: And the copying.

FIPP: Oh yes. The copying. You're a good girl, Hope Cladwell. I used to be one. Before I met your father.

HOPE: A good girl?

FIPP: You heard me. *(He pulls a wad of bills from his pocket and counts quietly to himself.)* . . . Six hundred and twenty-two. Six hundred and twenty-three. Just a few more.

HOPE: Daddy? Can I ask you a question?

CLADWELL: Sure, Hope darling. What is it?

HOPE: Do you believe in love?

(Pause.)

CLADWELL: Love? Why do you ask?

HOPE: Just wondering. I met this boy, you see—

(MCQUEEN, LOCKSTOCK, BARREL, and PENNY enter.)

MCQUEEN: Sorry to interrupt, Mister Cladwell. We've got a little problem.

PENNY: Caldwell. *(Musical sting.)* Long time, no see.

CLADWELL: Ms. Pennywise. *(Another musical sting.)*

(PENNY and CLADWELL share a long, meaningful look.)

McQUEEN: Anyway . . . it's about Public Amenity Number Nine, sir. The people there have rioted.

CLADWELL: Rioted?!

PENNY: They're peeing for free, Caldwell. I tried to stop them.

LOCKSTOCK: The assistant custodian is refusing to take people's money, sir. A young man by the name of Bobby Strong.

HOPE: Bobby Strong?

LOCKSTOCK: They've rescinded the Public Health Act.

McQUEEN: And the Water Preservation Act.

FIPP: Can they do that?!

McQUEEN: Strictly symbolic, sir. The crowd gathered there is an unthinkably small percentage of the population as a whole.

HOPE: What's happening, Daddy? I don't understand.

CLADWELL: I wouldn't expect a good and pure heart like yours to understand.

LOCKSTOCK: Mister Barrel and I are ready, Mister Cladwell. Just give the word.

FIPP: What did I tell you, Cladwell? It's a powder keg out there, and I have a very important plane to catch! Excuse me. *(He turns to go.)*

CLADWELL: Fipp! *(BARREL blocks his way.)* You're not going anywhere. Not until we nip this unpleasantness in the bud.

HOPE: Nip? How so?

CLADWELL: You're a Cladwell, Hope. What would you do if the very foundation of your life's work were threatened by the rabble-rousing son of a convicted criminal?

HOPE: Look deep into his heart and try to understand what made it pound so angrily.

CLADWELL: Angry, you say?! No one gets angry at me! Not without a beating!

HOPE: A beating? Oh, Daddy, beating people is wrong.

CLADWELL: Life is a beating! The sooner you learn that, the better.

HOPE: Then life is wrong.

CLADWELL: Embrace it. I have.

HOPE: Life should be beautiful.

CLADWELL: Life is many things. Look deeper, you'll see it. I do. *(Vamp for "Don't Be the Bunny" begins.)* I see it everywhere. *(He sings.)*

A little bunny in the meadow
Is nibbling grass without a care.
He's so delightful as he hops for you.
You say, "Hi, Bunny," and he stops for you.
You pull your trigger and he drops for you.
Goodbye, Bunny-boo;
Hello, rabbit stew!

Get me, boys?

UGC STAFF: You tell 'em, boss!

CLADWELL:

Don't be the bunny.
Don't be the stew.
Don't be the dinner.
You have better things to do.
It ain't no joke.
That's why it's funny.
So take your cue:
Don't be the bunny.
Don't be the bunny.

HOPE: But, Daddy, we're talking about people, not animals.

CLADWELL: People are animals, Hope darling.

HOPE: Animals with huge incisors and big floppy feet?

CLADWELL: Look closely, you'll see them. I do. I see them . . . everywhere. *(He sings.)*

A little bunny at a tollbooth.
He needs a measly fifty cents.
Our little bunny didn't plan ahead.
Poor bunny simply doesn't have the bread!
He begs for mercy, but gets jail instead.
Hasenpfeffer's in the air
As the bunny gets the chair!
See the moral, people?

UGC STAFF: Clear as day, boss!

CLADWELL:
Don't be the bunny.
Don't be the dope.
Don't be the loser.
You're much better than that, Hope!
You're born to pow'r.
You're in the money!
Advice to you—

MCQUEEN AND FIPP:
In re: the bunny—

CLADWELL:
Don't be the bunny!

HOPE: A little bunny at a tollbooth?

CLADWELL: You heard me.

HOPE: But, Daddy, bunnies don't drive cars.

CLADWELL: Oh, don't they?!

HOPE: No, actually, I don't think they do.

CLADWELL: Live long enough, Hope darling, you see . . . many things.

HOPE: Even a daughter doubting her father?

CLADWELL:
A little bunny in a shoe box.
He thinks he's found a brand-new home.
So snug and cozy on your closet floor,

And then you open up your closet door.
Now what's that bunny in my closet for?
With a mallet and some clippers,
You find out: new bunny slippers!
Grasp the message, staff?

UGC STAFF: Right behind you, boss!

CLADWELL AND STAFF:
Don't be the bunny.
Don't be the shoe.
You don't get stepped on.

CLADWELL:
No, the one who steps is you!

CLADWELL AND STAFF:
You're stepping up
To where it's sunny.
Step on the poor!
Don't be the bunny!
Don't be the bunny!
Wah, wah, wah, wah, wah!

CLADWELL: All right, everybody, get yourselves together! It's time we bagged ourselves a few rabbits! Let's go!

(All exit.)

Scene 6

The poorest, filthiest urinal in town. BOBBY, *with* JOSEPHINE's *help, is now in charge.* THE POOR *push eagerly toward the Amenity's entrance.*

BOBBY: One at a time! One at a time! Everyone will get a turn!

SOUPY SUE: Here's some cash, Bobby. Just for you.

BOBBY: Keep your cash, friend. And relieve yourself in happiness.

JOSEPHINE: A busy day so far. Busiest on record, if your books are right. How's the urinal holding out?

BOBBY: A little spillage, nothing to be concerned about. The people are happy, that's the main thing.

(A police whistle is heard in the distance.)

LITTLE BECKY TWO-SHOES: Police!

ROBBY THE STOCKFISH: Run!

BOBBY: Wait! Wait! Please, everyone, remain calm!

(The COPS *enter with* CLADWELL, MCQUEEN, FIPP, PENNY, *and* HOPE *in tow. They make their way to the gate.)*

LOCKSTOCK: It'll take a lot of explaining to keep us calm, Bobby Strong.

BOBBY: We've taken control of this amenity, Officers. The people here pee for free.

CLADWELL: That's my amenity, Officers. I want all of these people taken away.

*(*LITTLE SALLY *makes her way through the rebel mob to approach* LOCKSTOCK.*)*

LITTLE SALLY: Officer Lockstock, what's happening?

LOCKSTOCK: Why, it's the Act One finale, Little Sally. This is where Cladwell arrives to snuff out the uprising. It's a big song-and-dance number involving the entire cast.

LITTLE SALLY: Snuff out the uprising? But what about Bobby's dreams?

LOCKSTOCK: Well now, Little Sally, dreams only come true in happy musicals—and a few Hollywood movies—and this certainly isn't either one of those. No, dreams are meant to be crushed. It's nature's way.

LITTLE SALLY: This may not be a happy musical, Officer Lockstock, but it's still a musical. And when a little girl has been given as many lines as I have, there's still hope for dreams! *(She scrambles back to the mob.)*

HOPE: Bobby?!

BOBBY: Hope?!

HOPE: What are you doing, Bobby?! I told you to follow your heart, not seize an amenity!

BOBBY: I did follow my heart, Hope. Thanks to you.

PENNY: The amenity won't take much more of this uprising, Caldwell. Bobby's a sweet boy, but not sweet enough to sweeten that spillage, not by a long shot.

BOBBY: The amenity will take as much as it has to, Ms. Pennywise. The days of deprivation are over for these people.

THE POOR: Hooray!

CLADWELL: The days of deprivation have just begun if this madness continues a moment longer.

THE POOR: Ooooo!

BOBBY: Sure, Mister Cladwell, that's what you've been saying for twenty years. And for twenty years we've waited for the long-term solutions that never came. Well, we're done waiting, you see, for a new day has dawned today. A day of hope and happiness *(Musical vamp begins.)* when the idea of human dignity is more than just a forgotten notion, but a living, breathing reality. A day—this day—when the people pee for free, because the people are free!

THE POOR: Hooray!

BOBBY: *(Sings.)*
Free!
People are free!
How can a fee
Enslave us?
See
How we can be
Free from the chains
He gave us!

We're suffering now
Such lives of sorrow!

Don't give us tomorrow,
Just give us today!

THE POOR:
Free!
People are free!
How can a fee
Enslave us?
See
How we can be
Free from the chains
He gave us!

We're suffering now
Such lives of sorrow!
Don't give us tomorrow,
Just give us today!

BOBBY:
From ev'ry hill,
Ev'ry steeple,
Ring out the anthem
Of the people,
Making a new way,
Breaking the clouds of gray,
To sing of today!

BOBBY AND THE POOR:
Sing of today!
Sing of today,
Sing today,
Sing today,
Sing today!

PENNY: Uh, perhaps best to stay back here with your father, Hope dear. The police will want to charge soon.

BOBBY: Your father?

HOPE: Charge?! Daddy, these people need understanding, not brutality.

CLADWELL: On the contrary, Hope dear, a little brutality is exactly what these people need. Officer Lockstock!

HOPE: Daddy, wait. He only wants the people to be happy, isn't that worth something?

CLADWELL: Happy, you say?! Happy?! *(He sings.)*

So you want happy, Mister Strong?
Did you say happy, Mister Strong?
If they pee today, I'm sure they'll be
As happy as a pup!
With no rules and no more fees to pay,
Things would be looking up!
But too bad the water that we share
Could fit inside a cup!
What of tomorrow, Mister Strong?

BOBBY: But what of today?!

CLADWELL:

But what of tomorrow, Mister Strong?!
Think of tomorrow, Mister Strong!
Our resources are as fragile
As a newborn baby's skull!
With your actions you would gut the child
And leave a lifeless hull!
Could it be you're so shortsighted,
So insensitive, so dull?
Think of tomorrow, Mister Strong!

THE POOR: But what of today?!

CLADWELL AND CO.:

You are wrong, Mister Strong,
You and your socialistic throng!
If the people pee for free, they'll push
The system to the brink!

If today there's spillage, tell us how
Tomorrow will not stink!

CLADWELL:
If it's you and me, now, Mister Strong,
Which one of us will blink?

I say it's you, Mister Strong,
For on the subject of tomorrow—

CLADWELL AND CO.:
You are wrong!

CLADWELL: Officer Lockstock! Prepare your . . . man.

BOBBY: Everybody into the amenity! We'll be . . . relatively safer in there!

HOPE: Oh, Bobby, why didn't you tell me you were going to start a revolution?

BOBBY: Maybe for the same reason you didn't tell me you were a Cladwell.

HOPE: I'm the same girl I was last night.

BOBBY: The girl last night would have joined us by now, Hope.

HOPE: I can't fight against my father, Bobby.

BOBBY: And I can't not fight against him. So you can join us or you can stand aside.

HOPE: Stand aside?

BOBBY: You heard me.

HOPE: *(Sings.)*
Bobby, think!
You're standing on the brink!
You'll be arrested soon,
Perhaps as soon as noon,

And I could never bear
To see you taken where

The guilty peeers meet
The toilet judgment seat!

BOBBY:

You said
To follow your heart.
Here's where my heart leads.
Now I'll do my part
To banish all needs.

You made me to see,
Fantastic'lly clear.
When people pee free,
We've nothing to fear.

HOPE:

Give up now!
We'll find a way somehow
To help the people pee
Without a hefty fee.
But if you must persist
Being an anarchist,
My father's men will see
You're sent away from me!

You'll get Urinetown!

Bobby, you'll get
Urinetown!

Off you'll go to
Urinetown!

BOBBY:

Your words were like seeds,

At first they seemed mild.

They grew into deeds.

This riot's our child!

Sing of today, not tomorrow!

End their lives of sorrow!

Today!

Urinetown!

Today!

Urinetown!

Sing of today!

CLADWELL: You've picked a fight you can't win, today, Mister Strong! Your rabble is no match for my men.

JOSEPHINE: He's right, Bobby. They've got . . . one . . . two . . . Two men, and we're all so poor!

CLADWELL: Now release the girl. It's time you faced your punishment like a man.

BOBBY: Release?! No one's holding—

(The ghost of OLD MAN STRONG *and* TINY TOM *appear in the distance.)*

OLD MAN STRONG: Bobby! Bobby, reason with the woman! I'm a little short this morning!

TINY TOM: No shorter than yesterday. Unless I've grown.

(They disappear.)

LITTLE SALLY: You can punish our bodies, Mister Cladwell, but you can never punish our spirits!

SOUPY SUE: Punish our bodies?!

LITTLE BECKY TWO-SHOES: I never agreed to any punishment of my body!

CLADWELL: Oh, punishment is all you'll ever know . . . once you release the girl!!

THE POOR:
Bobby, help!
He'll turn our brains to kelp!
No matter what we do,
We're in a real bad stew!
Those cops look awful mean,

CLADWELL AND UGC STAFF:
You
are wrong, Mister Strong!
You
are wrong, Mister Strong!
Very

Like none we've ever seen!
When Cladwell gives the cue,
Our revolution's through!

wrong, Mister Strong!
You
are wrong, Mister Strong!

BOBBY:	THE POOR:	CLADWELL AND UGC STAFF:	HOPE:
Last night your words were like seeds.	*Bobby, please! There's no way to appease a raging maniac,*	*You are wrong, Mister Strong!*	
At first, they seemed mild.	*A real in-saniac! He's like a speeding train*	*You are wrong, Mister Strong!*	
They grew in-to deeds.	*caught in a hurricane, but he is in control,*	*Very wrong, Mister Strong!*	
This riot's our child!	*and he is on a roll!*	*You are wrong, Mister Strong!*	
The child is on fire.	*Cladwell's nuts! With no if's, and's, or but's! Yes, he's a real-live loon!*	*You are wrong, Mister Strong!*	*Oh Bob-by!*
He's hot as the sun!	*A freaking looney tune! And when he's done with us,*	*You are wrong, Mister Strong!*	*No, Bob-by!*
He'll burn like a	*we'll find we're on a bus bound for that*	*Very wrong, Mister Strong!*	*Oh Bob-by!*

pyre
till
freedom is
is
won!

unknown place
that we all
dread to face!

You are
wrong, Mister
Strong!

No,
Bob-
by!

ALL BUT BOBBY:
You'll / We'll get
Urinetown!

Bobby, you'll / we'll get
Urinetown!

Off you'll / we'll go to
Urinetown!

Urinetown!

Urinetown!

BOBBY:

Sing of today,
not tomorrow!

End their lives
of sorrow!

Today!

Today!

Sing of today!

(HOPE *and* BOBBY *embrace.*)

HOPE: So what'll it be, Bobby?

BOBBY: Looks like we're in a real tight spot, doesn't it?

HOPE: Your fellow revolutionaries seem to think so.

BOBBY: I suppose we should leave.

HOPE: Oh, Bobby, they'll never let you leave now.

(*The ghost of* OLD MAN STRONG *appears in the distance.*)

OLD MAN STRONG: Remember me, boys! Oh God, what have I done?! Remember me!!!

(*He disappears.*)

BOBBY: Not without you, they won't. Which is why you're coming with us.   •

The Musical

HOPE: Coming with you? I told you, Bobby, I won't fight against my father.

(BOBBY *clutches* HOPE *tighter.*)

BOBBY: And I told you I won't not fight against him.

HOPE: But how can I come with you and still not fight against my father unless . . . unless . . . oh dear God, Bobby, no!!!

BOBBY AND POOR:	CLADWELL AND CO.:
From ev'ry	
Hill,	*Wrong, Mister Strong!*
Ev'ry steeple,	*Think of tomorrow,*
	Mister Strong!
Ring out the anthem	*Our resources are as*
	Fragile
Of the people	*As a newborn baby's skull!*
Making a	*With your*
New way,	*Actions you would gut the*
Breaking the	*Child and*
Clouds of gray	*Leave a lifeless hull!*
	A lifeless hull,
To sing of today!	*Mister Strong!*
	You're very dull,
	Mister Strong!
Sing of today!	*Disperse your throng,*
	Mister Strong!
	Disperse your throng,
	And end your song,
Sing of today!	*And end your song,*
	Mister Strong!
	You're wrong,
	Mister Strong!
Sing today!	*You're wrong,*
	Mister Strong!

Sing today!	*You're wrong!*
	Mister Strong!
Sing today!	*You're wrong!*

BOBBY: Keep your men back, Cladwell! We've got your daughter and we're not letting her go!

HOPE: Bobby, what are you—

JOSEPHINE: *(Pulling her away.)* In the name of the sky, you're coming with us!

BOBBY: We're walking out of here, Mister Cladwell, and you're going to let us! That is, if you care about your daughter.

CLADWELL: You're making a terrible mistake, Mister Strong.

PENNY: Let the girl go, Bobby, she's done nothing wrong!

BOBBY: Don't let go of the girl. And follow me!

LOCKSTOCK: Boss, what do we do?!

CLADWELL: Seize them!

PENNY: No!

CLADWELL: Don't let them get away!

HOPE: Help me!

PENNY: Help her!

BOBBY: Now run, everybody! Run for your lives! RUN!!

(General mayhem, first in real time, then in slow motion. BOBBY, JOSEPHINE, *and the rest of* THE POOR *escape with* HOPE *as a hostage. Everyone sings as* LOCKSTOCK *explains.)*

WOMEN:	MEN:	LOCKSTOCK:
Urinetown!		Well, that's it for Act One.
	Urinetown!	As you can see, the rebel
Urinetown!		poor are making their get-
	Urinetown!	away with Hope as a hos-
Urinetown!		tage. The rest of us have
	Urinetown!	been thrown into confu-

Urinetown!

Urinetown!

Urinetown!

Urine-!

Urinetown! *Urinetown!*

Urinetown! *Urinetown!*

sion because—well, because we're all moving so damned slowly. So we don't get to catch them. Not yet. Enjoy intermission, and see you—shortly!

Scene 1

Montage. "What is Urinetown?" vamp plays in the background. Above the stage hangs a sign that reads A SECRET HIDEOUT. OFFICER LOCKSTOCK enters to address the audience.

LOCKSTOCK: Well, hello there. And welcome—to Act Two! Things have changed here a bit since last we saw each other, so I'll bring you up to speed on a few things. As you may remember, the rebel poor under Bobby's leadership kidnapped Hope and used her as a shield to escape due punishment from my . . . man. Word has it they're holed up in some secret hideout somewhere. Perhaps this one—here.

(Lights cross to the rebel hideout. HOPE sits bound to a chair and gagged. THE POOR are becoming increasingly anxious.)

SOUPY SUE: Where the hell is Bobby?! And Little Sally?! And Old Ma Strong?! They should have been back by now.

HOT BLADES HARRY: Ah, who are we kiddin'? The police probably nabbed them hours ago. It's just a matter of time before our whereabouts are tortured out of them. And then it'll be off to Urinetown for the lot of us.

TINY TOM: Wha-what's it like, do you think?

HOT BLADES HARRY: Urinetown? Don't even ask.

ROBBY THE STOCKFISH: No one knows for sure.

HOT BLADES HARRY: I got my suspicions.

TINY TOM: Oh yeah?

LITTLE BECKY TWO-SHOES: Sure, kid, everyone's got suspicions.
(She sings.)

What is Urinetown?
Urinetown's the end!
Swift and brutal punishment—
No need now to pretend!

HOT BLADES HARRY:
The trapdoor's sprung and then you're hung,
And when they cut you down,
They'll box you up and ship you out
And call it Urinetown!

ALL:
They'll box you up and ship you out
And call it Urinetown!
Town!
Town!
Town!
Town!

THE POOR:
Dance?
No!
Never do they dance!
Those people down in Urinetown, they never get the chance!
Dancing, forget it!
Never, nada, nope!
Unless it's at the bottom of a rope!

HOT BLADES HARRY: So don't get your hopes up. And I say if they're not back soon, we give it to her like her father was gonna give it to us.

(Lights cross back to LOCKSTOCK.*)*

LOCKSTOCK: People hear lots of things about Urinetown, of course, and that's just the way we like it. For example, a little boy once asked me, "Is Urinetown actually a nice place to live? Gingerbread houses along golden, frothy canals? Like Venice, but different?" I didn't say yes. I didn't say no either.

(CLADWELL, MCQUEEN, *and* FIPP *enter.*)

CLADWELL: I want them found, damn it! I want my daughter released and I want Bobby Strong punished!

LOCKSTOCK: We're working round the clock, sir. But as the sign says, it is a secret hideout, so—

CLADWELL: Enough of your excuses, Lockstock! You've got weapons! Use them!

LOCKSTOCK: But, sir—

CLADWELL: *(Sings.)*

What is Urinetown?
Urinetown's a tool,
An instrument of power
To enforce my iron rule!
So send your troops to all the stoops
And let them understand,
If Hope is not returned,
It's Urinetown for all the land!

ALL:

If Hope is not returned,
It's Urinetown for all the land!
Land!
Land!
Land!
Land!

CLADWELL:

Dance?
Dance?
Do they think I'll dance?
Those people with my daughter want to
Make me change my stance!
Stance-dance, forget it!
Never, nada, nein!
I'll teach them not to take from me what's mine!

MCQUEEN: We should hurry, sir. The Emergency Planning Quorum is waiting.

CLADWELL: Yes, of course. The Quorum.

(They exit. Lights cross to BOBBY *and* JOSEPHINE, *now elsewhere in the city.)*

JOSEPHINE: That was a close one, Bobby. I thought Barrel saw us there for sure.

BOBBY: We'll have to keep on our toes, Ma. At least until we've distributed the rest of these memos to the other assistant custodians around the city.

JOSEPHINE: Do you think they'll join us?

BOBBY: Hard to say. They're scared like we used to be scared, but if it's true what they say about everyone having a heart, they'll have to join us. *(He sings.)*

What is Urinetown?
Urinetown's a lie,
A means to keep the poor in check
Until the day they die!
I did not shirk their dirty work,
But things are different now.
We'll fight for right with all our might
Until we win somehow!

BOBBY AND JOSEPHINE:
We'll fight for right with all our might
Until we win somehow!
How!
How!
How!
How!

BOBBY:
Dance!
Dance!
Listen to it dance!

My heart is like a stallion racing through a great expanse!
Canyons of freedom, that's where it will waltz,
Performing coronary somersaults!

JOSEPHINE: Your heart is like a stallion?

(A police whistle is heard in the distance.)

BOBBY: I'll explain along the way, Ma. C'mon, let's go.

(They exit. Lights cross to LOCKSTOCK, *who's just nabbed* LITTLE SALLY.*)*

LOCKSTOCK: Where are they hiding, Little Sally?! Tell me and I'll see things go easy on you.

LITTLE SALLY: Easy on me?! You mean like sending me to the nice part of Urinetown?!

LOCKSTOCK: That can be arranged.

LITTLE SALLY: Save it for one of your other stoolies, Officer Lockstock. My heart's with the rebellion. And besides, the way I see it, I'm already in Urinetown. We all are. Even you.

*(*LOCKSTOCK *loosens his grip.)*

LOCKSTOCK: Me? In Urinetown?

LITTLE SALLY: Sure. The way I see it, Urinetown isn't so much a place as it is a metaphysical place. *(She sings.)*

What is Urinetown?
Urinetown is here!
It's the town wherever
People learn to live in fear.
So look around, you've fin'lly found
The place you asked about,
For Urinetown is your town
If you're hopeless, down-and-out!

ALL:

For Urinetown is your town
If you're hopeless, down-and-out!

*(*LOCKSTOCK *sings alone while* LITTLE SALLY *scrambles off.)*

The Musical

LOCKSTOCK:

For Urinetown is your town
If you're hopeless, down-and-out!

ALL:

Out!

Out!

Out!

Out!

(LOCKSTOCK looks around and sees that LITTLE SALLY has escaped.)

LOCKSTOCK: Where'd she go?! Damn it. *(He turns to go, but before he leaves—)* Welcome back, everybody. And enjoy— what's left of the show! Little Sally . . . Little Sally . . . what did you mean by "metaphysical"?

ALL:

Hey!

Scene 2

The secret hideout. THE POOR *have just about lost it.*

HOT BLADES HARRY: I say five more seconds and then we let her have the rope. Five . . . Four . . . Three, two, one!

(LITTLE SALLY enters.)

LITTLE SALLY: Geez, that was a close one. Cops crawlin' all over the place.

LITTLE BECKY TWO-SHOES: Little Sally! Where the hell have you been?!

LITTLE SALLY: Spyin' near the tower, is all. Cladwell and Fipp and Ms. Pennywise, they was all meetin' up there. Some kind of—I don't know what you want to call it—a quorum of some kind.

HOT BLADES HARRY: That's it, she gets the rope.

LITTLE SALLY: The rope?

LITTLE BECKY TWO-SHOES: String her up!

LITTLE SALLY: Wait a minute! You can't just give her the rope!

HOT BLADES HARRY: Why not?!

LITTLE SALLY: Because killin' her would make us no better than them.

LITTLE BECKY TWO-SHOES: Haven't you heard, Little Sally? We are no better than them. In fact, we're worse.

LITTLE SALLY: Worse?!

(Vamp begins for "Snuff That Girl.")

HOT BLADES HARRY: Whaddaya think they talk about in those quorums they got up there—how good we are?! So listen up now! Any second those cops are gonna bust in here and bust us up like a bunch of overripe cantaloupes! So I say as long as our juice has gotta spill—all over this floor, here—her juice has gotta spill, too! Cladwell juice! Then we'll see who's better than who. *(He sings.)*

Look at her there,
All bound up, gagged and tied,
With her head full of hair
And her heart full of pride.
Well, boys, I've had enough
Of each arrogant curl.
Bing! Bang! Boom! Let's get tough,
Playin' rough.
Snuff that girl.

LITTLE SALLY: "Snuff that girl"? But killing people is wrong!

LITTLE BECKY TWO-SHOES: Then why does it feel so right? *(She sings.)*

Look at us here
In a hole, on the lam,
With our hearts full of fear.
What a rip! What a sham!
You know cops will be here
Bustin' heads mighty quick.

HOT BLADES HARRY:

But we'll beat them to the punch
When we snuff out that chick!

LITTLE BECKY TWO-SHOES:

We tried doin' what we should.

HOT BLADES HARRY:

Wasn't glad.

LITTLE BECKY TWO-SHOES:

Then we learned that feelin' good

HOT BLADES HARRY:

Means doin' bad.

HOT BLADES HARRY AND LITTLE BECKY TWO-SHOES:

Nuts, they fall close,
So they say, to the tree.
Looky here, here's an a-
Corn from Cladwell I see.
I say she is the nut,
And of course, we're the squirrel.
She is what we saved for winter,
So let's snuff that girl.

HOT BLADES HARRY:

Bing!

TINY TOM:

Bing!

LITTLE BECKY TWO-SHOES:

A-bing bang!

SOUPY SUE:

Bing bang!

HOT BLADES HARRY:

A-bing bang boom!

ROBBY THE STOCKFISH:

Boom!

BILLY BOY BILL:

Boom!

HOT BLADES HARRY:

Yeah!

LITTLE BECKY TWO-SHOES:

Okay now, snuff!

BILLY BOY BILL:

Snuff the girl!

LITTLE BECKY TWO-SHOES:

Yeah!

SOUPY SUE AND BILLY BOY BILL:

Snuff the girl!

TINY TOM AND ROBBY THE STOCKFISH:

Snuff her!

HOT BLADES HARRY AND LITTLE BECKY TWO-SHOES:

Oh yeah, now go!

ROBBY THE STOCKFISH:

Snuff the girl!

HOT BLADES HARRY AND LITTLE BECKY TWO-SHOES:

Yeah!

BILLY BOY, ROBBY, TINY TOM, HOT BLADES HARRY:

Snuff the girl!

ALL:

Yeah, snuff the girl!
(Dance break.)

ALL:

This is the end.
Roll the dice, place your bets.
In this mis'rable world,
That's as good as it gets.
So now, let's live it up.
Eat the oyster and the pearl.

And let's get this party jumpin',
Really get it pumpin'.
Let's get this party jumpin'.
Yeah, let's snuff that—
Snuff that girl!

TINY TOM: Let's bring our message of hate to the entire world!

HOT BLADES HARRY: Easy, friend, a message like ours works best under extremely unbalanced circumstances.

LITTLE BECKY TWO-SHOES: Such as we have right here?

HOT BLADES HARRY: Exactly. Now, get the rope.

TINY TOM: That's right, the rope.

(BOBBY and JOSEPHINE enter the secret hideout unseen.)

LITTLE BECKY TWO-SHOES: String her up. That's the answer. String up the strumpet daughter of the criminal urinal chain owner Cladwell!

SOUPY SUE: Kill her!

ROBBY THE STOCKFISH: Hang her!

LITTLE BECKY TWO-SHOES: Kill her!

BOBBY: Enough!

THE POOR: Whaa—?!

LITTLE SALLY: Bobby Strong.

BOBBY: No one's going to be killing anyone around here.

HOT BLADES HARRY: Why not?

JOSEPHINE: Because she's our security blanket, that's why!

SOUPY SUE: But we're so afraid, Bobby. Killing her might make us feel powerful for a moment.

BOBBY: Friends, I know you're afraid. But this has got to be about more than just revenge and the vicarious thrill of stringing someone up who can't defend herself.

LITTLE BECKY TWO-SHOES: But why? We want to hang her as revenge for her father's crimes.

LITTLE SALLY: I think he's just in love with her, that's what I think.

BOBBY: Maybe I am.

ALL: Whaa—?!

BOBBY: And maybe I made a promise up there. A promise that from this day forward, no man would be denied his essential humanity due to the condition of his pocketbook. That no man in need would be ignored by another with the means to help him. Here and now, from this day forward, because of you, and you, and you, we will look into the faces of our fellow men and see not only a brother, but a sister as well.

HOT BLADES HARRY: What is that supposed to mean?

SOUPY SUE: When did he say that?

TINY TOM: I don't remember him saying that.

LITTLE BECKY TWO-SHOES: All I remember him saying was "Run! Run for your lives! Run!"

BOBBY: Well, that was in the heat of battle. And in the heat—the actual hotness of battle—the cry of freedom sounds something like *(He sings.)*
Run, freedom, run!
Freedom, run away!
My friends, you have to run,
Run-a, run-a, run.
Freedom, run away!

That freedom sun
Will shine someday.
Till then you better run,
Run-a, run-a, run.
Freedom, run away!

TINY TOM: I'm frightened!

BOBBY: As well you should be. Freedom is scary; it's a blast of cool wind that burns your face to wake you up.

TINY TOM: Literally?!

(Pause.)

BOBBY: Yes. *(He sings.)*
There's a trickle of sweat—

THE POOR:
There's a trickle of sweat—

BOBBY:
Drippin' in your ear—

THE POOR:
Drippin' in your ear—

BOBBY:	**THE POOR:**
But still, you gotta run,	*Ah—*
Run-a, run-a, run.	
Freedom, run away!	

THE POOR:
Run, run away!

BOBBY:	**THE POOR:**
So now, don't you fret,	*Ah—*
And never fear!	
Till freedom's	

BOBBY AND THE POOR:
Won, won-a, won-a, won.

BOBBY:
Freedom, run away!

THE POOR:
Run, freedom, run!

BOBBY:
There's a great, big Cladwell on your tail!

THE POOR:
Run, freedom, run!

BOBBY:

And he's put his henchmen on your trail!

THE POOR:

Run, freedom, run!

BOBBY:

I'm simply layin' out the fac's for you.
Great, big Cladwell's makin' tracks for you.
Ain't no time to relax for you—

BOBBY AND THE POOR:

Run, freedom, run!

BOBBY:

Run, freedom, run!

THE POOR:

Run, freedom, run!
Run, freedom, run!

BOBBY:

Freedom, run away!

THE POOR:

Freedom, run away!
Freedom, run away!

BOBBY AND THE POOR:

My friends, you have to run,
Run-a, run-a, run.
Freedom, run away!

THE POOR:

Freedom, run away!
Freedom, run away!
Freedom, run away!

BOBBY AND THE POOR:

That freedom sun,
That freedom sun
Will shine someday.

BOBBY: *. . . Three, four!*

BOBBY AND THE POOR:
Till then you better
Run, run-a-freedom, run.
Freedom, run away.

BOBBY:
Run, freedom, run!
Freedom, run away!
My friends, you
Have to run,
Run-a, run-a, run.
Freedom, run away!

THE POOR:
Hallelujah!
Hallelujah!

Ah—

THE POOR:
Run, Hallelu!
BOBBY:
That freedom sun!
THE POOR:
Freedom sun!
BOBBY:
Will shine someday.
THE POOR:
Some sweet day!
BOBBY AND THE POOR:
Till then you better
Run, run-a, run-a, run,
Run-a, run-a, run.
Hallelujah!
THE POOR:
Freedom, run!
BOBBY:
With the wind in your hair,
You'll run to freedom glory.

THE POOR:

Freedom sun!

BOBBY:

That freedom sun will shine
All over our freedom story!
I said freedom—
I said freedom—
I said, freedom, run.
Freedom, run
Away!

THE POOR:

Run, freedom, run!
Run, freedom!
Freedom, run away!

(THE POOR continue backup vocals under the following.)

LITTLE SALLY: What do we do now?

JOSEPHINE: The police will be on the lookout for us, that's for sure.

BOBBY: When the time comes, we fight the police!

SOUPY SUE: But how?!

(Backup vocals trail off as THE POOR realize what BOBBY's suggesting.)

BOBBY: With blood! Guts! Brains, if we have to! It may take years! And some of us will almost certainly not make it through the revolution alive! Maybe all of us! But fight on we will, for all the decades necessary, to claim freedom for the people of this land!!

(Pause. PENNY enters, unseen.)

TINY TOM: Decades?

LITTLE BECKY TWO-SHOES: How about a real plan?

PENNY: I've got a real plan.

ALL: Whaa—?!

BOBBY: Ms. Pennywise? How did you find us?

PENNY: I had a feeling you'd be here. No one knows the sewer system like you do, Bobby.

BOBBY: Or you.

PENNY: Cladwell would like to talk to you, Bobby.

BOBBY: What about?

PENNY: He wants to discuss the situation with you man-to-man. He says he now understands how unhappy the people of this community have become and he wants to work out a solution with you. Peacefully.

TINY TOM: Now there's a shortcut.

SOUPY SUE: That'll save us on the decades of struggle!

JOSEPHINE: But can we trust him?

PENNY: Mister Cladwell doesn't want a fight, Mrs. Strong. He just wants his amenities up and running, smooth and natural. That's all he's ever wanted.

BOBBY: What do you think, Little Sally?

LITTLE SALLY: I think it might be difficult for your love to grow with Hope tied to that chair for the rest of her life.

(BOBBY thinks a moment.)

BOBBY: All right, I'll go.

(General commotion.)

JOSEPHINE: Bobby, no! What if it's a trick?!

BOBBY: That's just a chance I'll have to take.

ALL: *[Gasp!]*

PENNY: What about the girl?

JOSEPHINE: She stays here. Any funny business and she gets it. You tell that to Cladwell.

PENNY: Sure, I'll tell him. Likewise with the girl. Give it to her and we give it to him. Get me?

BOBBY: We'll be careful.

PENNY: Now, stay calm, Hope darling. We'll have you out of this in no time.

(PENNY *exits.* BOBBY *takes off* HOPE's *gag.*)

HOPE: Hello, Bobby.

BOBBY: Hello, Hope.

HOPE: So this is the bright, new day you were telling me about.

BOBBY: I don't blame you for being angry with me, Hope. But your father gave us no choice.

HOPE: They may not have taught me much at the Most Expensive University in the World, but they taught me this much: kidnapping people is wrong.

BOBBY: Really? They taught you that there?

(*Pause.*)

HOPE: I thought we had something special together, Bobby.

BOBBY: We do have something special together, Hope. But until freedom rules the people of this land instead of fear, love has about as much chance as a baby bunny drowning in a vat of boiling water.

HOPE: Maybe less.

(*Pause.*)

BOBBY: I didn't mean to drag you into all this, Hope.

HOPE: And I didn't mean to . . . Oh, I guess I don't know what I meant to do.

BOBBY: Look to your heart, Hope. I think the answer to what you want is waiting for you there, deep down, somewhere among the tissues. (*He exits.*)

HOPE: Wait a minute, when will I see you again? (*She sings.*)
When darkness surrounds you,
And you've lost your way,
You have your own compass
That turns night to day,
And it's even with you
Before you depart.
Be still, hear it beating,

The Musical

It's leading you.
Follow your—
Oh, Bobby.

Scene 3

The offices of Urine Good Company. CLADWELL, FIPP, *and* UGC
STAFF *receive* PENNY *and* BOBBY.

CLADWELL: You've caused a lot of excitement over the past few
days, Mister Strong. Gotten a lot of people riled up.

BOBBY: This is just the beginning, Mister Cladwell. The people
have only just begun to fight.

CLADWELL: Keeping my daughter confined against her will—is
that how the people fight?

BOBBY: They fight by any means necessary.

MRS. MILLENNIUM: The streets are still ours, Mister Strong. Your
people are just holed up in some underground sewer.

BOBBY: They'll be up.

*(*LOCKSTOCK *and* BARREL *rush in, truncheons in hand.)*

LOCKSTOCK: Sorry to interrupt, Mister Cladwell. There's a dis-
turbance over at Public Amenity Number Thirty-two, Number Fifteen as well. Word's begun to spread.

BARREL: People have gathered at all the rest. They're waiting to
see what young Bobby will do.

LOCKSTOCK: After he meets with you, of course.

CLADWELL: Of course. *(He considers* BOBBY.*)* Mister McQueen!
*(*MCQUEEN *places a suitcase on* CLADWELL'*s desk.)* Do you remember the Stink Years, Mister Strong? The first years when
the water table started to drop and then just kept on drop-
ping? No one thought they had much time then, and many of
us did . . . questionable things, much like the things that are

happening right now. There was the looting, of course, and the hoarding. Riots broke out like there was no tomorrow, for there was no tomorrow, but there is always a tomorrow if you're tough enough to cling to it. Which is why I've asked you here tonight.

(MCQUEEN *opens the suitcase, revealing piles and piles of cash.*)

ALL: Ooooooooo.

CLADWELL: Some people see me as an . . . evil man.

ALL: Noo! / How awful! / Oh, Mister Cladwell! / Etc.

CLADWELL: But the truth is, I'm no more evil than you or Ms. Pennywise or any of those poor people you insist on trying to lead. I'm only a simple man trying to cling to tomorrow. Every day. By any means necessary.

(BOBBY *fingers the cash.*)

BOBBY: And what happens when the drought is over?

CLADWELL: Over? (*All except* BOBBY *chuckle.*) Well, we can always hope, I suppose. But until then our regimen of controlling consumption through the regulating mechanism of cash must continue.

BOBBY: Ah yes, the regulating mechanism of cash.

(CLADWELL *puts his arm around* BOBBY.)

CLADWELL: Bobby, I want you to have this cash. And I want you to tell the people that the powers that be grant full amnesty to those involved in this week's criminal activities as long as they're willing to return to the improved fee schedule as authorized by the Legislature. Don't let it happen again, and have a good time in Rio.

BOBBY: So many tomorrows.

CLADWELL: Yes.

BOBBY: But I'm afraid my conscience will cost you more than a pile of cash, Mister Cladwell.

PENNY: Bobby, it really is an awful lot of cash.

BOBBY: Free access is the only "cash" I'm interested in.

CLADWELL: I thought we had an understanding, Bobby.

BOBBY: Then understand this: If there truly is a way to that bright, new day, we'll find it together. All of us, not just the wealthy few. And that means free access.

CLADWELL: Free access is impossible.

BOBBY: Then that's what I'll tell the people. *(He turns to go.)*

CLADWELL: Stop! *(LOCKSTOCK and BARREL block his exit.)* We'll not return to the Stink Years, Mister Strong. I'll not allow it.

PENNY: Caldwell, what are you doing?!

CLADWELL: I've spent a lifetime building this company, paying off the police, bribing the political elite, and snuffing out popular resistance as if it were a naughty baby bunny in the palm of my hand. My right hand. I've centralized all power to a pinpoint spot—right here! Between these two ears! And I'm not going to allow some dreamy-eyed boy who can't remember the Stink Years to ruin all that! Seize him!

(LOCKSTOCK and BARREL seize BOBBY.)

PENNY: Don't do it, Caldwell! There's no telling what they'll do to the girl!

CLADWELL: That's just a chance I'll have to take.

ALL: *[Gasp!]*

MRS. MILLENNIUM: He really is as evil as they say.

CLADWELL: You think just because I love my daughter I'll stop clinging to tomorrow?!

PENNY: Caldwell, what are you saying?!

(Two UGC EXECUTIVES step forward to restrain PENNY.)

CLADWELL: I closed my heart to love once, I can do it again! *(Vamp for "Why Did I Listen to That Man?" begins.)* To Urinetown with him, then! With all haste, Officer Lockstock! With all haste!

BOBBY: You lied to us, Cladwell! CLADWELL!

(The COPS drag BOBBY off, CLADWELL exits with his entourage. Begin montage. PENNY, still restrained by the UGC EXECUTIVES, sings.)

PENNY:

Why did I listen to that man?
Why did I listen to the nature of his plan?
And when he talked,
I should have balked,
I should have walked,
I should have ran!
Why did I listen to that man?

(She is dragged off. Outside the UGC headquarters building: CLAD-
WELL, MCQUEEN, DR. BILLEAUX, MRS. MILLENNIUM, *and* FIPP *enter.)*

CLADWELL: *(To* MCQUEEN*)* You, get word to police headquarters;
we'll need all hands on deck tonight. *(*MCQUEEN EXITS. *To* BIL-
LEAUX, MILLENNIUM, *then again to* BILLEAUX*)* You, you, and you,
stay with me! We'll see about these little "disturbances." And Fipp!

FIPP: Yes, Cladwell?

CLADWELL: Assemble the Legislature. I want full authority for
the coming crackdown.

FIPP: And dirty my hands with this bad business? Not on your
life.

CLADWELL: Don't kid yourself, Fipp. Your hands are as filthy as a
child's after sandbox time. But don't worry, you can wash
them soon enough! Wash them by the banks of the Rio del
Rio. Now go! *(To* BILLEAUX, MILLENNIUM, *then again to* BIL-
LEAUX*)* You, you, and you! Come with me!

(He rushes off with BILLEAUX *and* MILLENNIUM *in tow.* FIPP *sings.)*

FIPP:

Why did I listen to that crook?
A little bribe in cash is all it really took.
That's how that craven
Toilet maven
Made me cave in.
I'm a schnook!
Why did I listen to that crook?

(He rushes off. Somewhere on the way to the UGC headquarters building rooftop: LOCKSTOCK *and* BARREL *enter with* BOBBY, *now blindfolded and bound at the wrists.)*

BOBBY: You lied to us, Cladwell! You told us one thing, then you did another! That's what you did, Cladwell! That's what you did!

LOCKSTOCK: Come on then, young Bobby. You can't keep screaming all the way down to Urinetown.

BOBBY: But Hope, she's still with the others. What happens to me happens to her.

LOCKSTOCK: What happens to you happens to all of us sooner or later.

BARREL: Rather later than sooner, I'd say.

BOBBY: But not to Hope! Oh, please, not to Hope!

*(*LOCKSTOCK *and* BARREL *sing.)*

LOCKSTOCK AND BARREL:
Now we've fin'lly got you.
Now you're in our claws,
Captured in our city
Of laws.

There's no trial or jury,
Nothing to discuss.
Now the law is speaking
Through us.

You'll get Urinetown!
Off with you to Urinetown!
Away with you to Urinetown!
Now, no more fuss.
(They drag BOBBY *off. A street corner:* PENNY *is dragged on by two* UGC EXECUTIVES. *Lights also up on* HOPE, *still in the secret hideout, bound to a chair.)*

PENNY: Let go of me! I have to save Hope!

UGC EXECUTIVE #1: There's no saving Hope now, Ms. Penny-wise.

UGC EXECUTIVE #2: There may be no saving you.

PENNY: Oh no?! Then take that! And that! And this! And a few of these!

(She fights audibly with her captors. HOPE *sings.)*

HOPE:
Why did I listen to that boy?
He spoke of hopes and dreams.
It filled me with such joy.
How can I know
He loved me so?
Was it for show?
Was I his toy?
Why did I listen to that boy?

*(*PENNY *escapes, the* UGC EXECUTIVES *chase after her. The UGC headquarters building rooftop:* LOCKSTOCK *and* BARREL *enter with* BOBBY.)*

BOBBY: So what's it like, this Urinetown that I've heard so much about?

BARREL: Perhaps better for us to "show" you.

*(*BOBBY *bumps into the rooftop edging. He feels around.)*

BOBBY: What's this? Where are we?

BARREL: You, my boy, stand on the very threshold to a new world.

LOCKSTOCK: The door is in front of you. Step through and Urinetown awaits.

BOBBY: Door? More like . . . a railing. And pigeons. A rooftop?

BARREL: And a drop.

LOCKSTOCK: A decisive drop.

BOBBY: I guess I still don't understand.

BARREL: Never fear, the time of understanding is at hand!

(LOCKSTOCK rips off BOBBY's blindfold.)

LOCKSTOCK: Welcome, then! To the very gates of Urinetown itself!

(BOBBY stares awestruck at the spectacle. LOCKSTOCK and BARREL laugh maniacally. PENNY, now somewhere else in the city, appears. She sings with HOPE, who is still tied to her chair in the secret hideout.)

PENNY:

Why did I listen to that cad?

HOPE:

Why did I listen to my dad?

HOPE AND PENNY:

I went to work for him.
He said he was so glad.

HOPE:

Was he sincere?

PENNY:

Well, now it's clear—

HOPE:

And now I fear—

HOPE AND PENNY:

That I've been had!
Why did I listen to

(FIPP, not far from the UGC headquarters building, appears. He sings with the others.)

FIPP:	PENNY:	LOCKSTOCK AND BARREL:	BOBBY:	HOPE:
That crook,				
That crook,	*That cad,*	*This is Urinetown!*		
That crook,	*That cad,*		*My heart,*	
That	*That cad,*	*Dead ahead it's*	*My heart,*	*My dad,*
crook,	*That cad,*	*Urinetown!*	*My heart,*	*My dad,*
That	*That cad,*		*My heart,*	*My dad,*

crook,	*That cad,*		*My heart,*	*My dad,*
That	*That cad,*	*You must go to*	*My heart,*	*My dad,*
crook,	*That cad,*	*Urinetown!*	*My heart,*	*My dad,*
That	*That cad,*		*My heart,*	*My dad,*
crook,	*That cad,*	*Urinetown!*	*My heart,*	*My dad,*
That	*That cad,*		*My heart,*	*My dad,*
crook,	*That cad,*	*Urinetown!*	*My heart,*	*My dad,*
Crook!	*Cad!*		*Heart!*	*Dad!*

ALL:

Urinetown!

(All repeat refrain "Urinetown" under following dialogue.)

BOBBY: Look, there's Public Amenity Number Forty-seven! And the Legislature! And . . . and my boyhood home! Why, we're just standing on top of the UGC headquarters building. And this . . . this is our town!

LOCKSTOCK: Yes. Yes, it is.

BOBBY: How could it be that we're in our town and in Urinetown at the same time . . . unless . . . unless . . . dear God, no! You couldn't have!

BARREL: Over you go, then.

BOBBY: Wait a minute, you're just going to throw me off this roof and that's supposed to be Urinetown?! Death is Urinetown?!

LOCKSTOCK: That's one interpretation.

(LOCKSTOCK and BARREL sing in counterpoint with BOBBY as HOPE, FIPP, and PENNY sing "Ah.")

BOBBY:	**LOCKSTOCK AND BARREL:**
Why did I listen to my heart?	
	There's no trial or jury!
I heard its call and made this revolution start!	
	Nothing to discuss!

So let the throng take up my
   song. Make Cladwell see that he is wrong!   Now the law is
Why did I listen to my heart?   speaking through us!

*(*BOBBY *now sings solo as* LOCKSTOCK *and* BARREL *join* HOPE, FIPP, *and* PENNY *singing "Ah.")*

BOBBY:
Why did I listen to my heart?
I heard its call and made this revolution start.
So let the throng
Take up my song.
Make Cladwell see that he is wrong!

BOBBY, HOPE, PENNY, FIPP, LOCKSTOCK, BARREL:
Why did I / he listen to that—
Why did I / he listen to that—

PENNY:
Cad?

HOPE:
Dad?

BOBBY, HOPE, PENNY, FIPP, LOCKSTOCK, BARREL:
Bad!
Why did I / he listen to my / his—

*(*LOCKSTOCK *and* BARREL *throw* BOBBY *off the edge.)*

BOBBY: Hearrrrrrrrrrrrrrrtttttt!!!!!!!

*(*LOCKSTOCK *and* BARREL *watch him fall. After a moment . . .)*

LOCKSTOCK: A shovel and a mop, Mister Barrel. You know the
   drill.

Scene 4

The secret hideout. THE POOR *guard* HOPE, *still bound to the chair and gagged. All wait anxiously for* BOBBY *to return.*

LITTLE BECKY TWO-SHOES: What's taking them so long?

SOUPY SUE: They should have reached an agreement by now. Cladwell's not one to dillydally.

TINY TOM: All night the sirens and the screams. Maybe they're celebrating?

JOSEPHINE: Bobby won't let us down. He's a good boy, my Bobby Strong. If anyone can find the way to freedom, he can.

HOT BLADES HARRY: Otherwise we kill the girl. Right? That is the plan, isn't it?

JOSEPHINE: Let's not get ahead of ourselves now, shall we?

(LITTLE SALLY enters.)

JOSEPHINE: Little Sally? What's going on up there?

LITTLE SALLY: It's . . . it's . . .

JOSEPHINE: Yes?

LITTLE SALLY: I saw Bobby.

JOSEPHINE: Yes?

LITTLE SALLY: I . . . I don't think the meeting went very well.

JOSEPHINE: Why do you say that?

LITTLE SALLY: Well, they threw him off a building.

(Pause.)

JOSEPHINE: What are you saying, Little Sally? Who threw who off a building?

LITTLE SALLY: Bobby. The policemen. They threw him off a building.

JOSEPHINE: The police threw Bobby off a building?

SOUPY SUE: They couldn't have done such a thing; we have Cladwell's daughter.

LITTLE SALLY: Well, they did.

TINY TOM: Is . . . is he all right?

LITTLE SALLY: Um . . .

JOSEPHINE: Well, is he?!

(LITTLE SALLY breaks down.)

LITTLE SALLY: Oh, Bobby. The policemen came soon enough, but not before I heard his last words.

ROBBY THE STOCKFISH: His last words?

LITTLE SALLY: That's right. *(She points to HOPE.)* It was about her.

(Vamp for "Tell Her I Love Her" begins. Pause.)

SOUPY SUE: Well, what were they?!

LITTLE SALLY: They were . . . *(She sings.)*
Tell her I love her,
Tell her I'll always be with her,
And I will see her in a better place,
Where hope is always new.

Ours was a short time.
Ours was a love that never bloomed.
Yet in that love there lives a brand-new hope
That's calling out to you.

Its call is soft and gentle, tame and fine.
It's docile and benign—
(The ghost of BOBBY suddenly appears in the distance and sings.)

BOBBY:
A pickle in the brine.
What did I say? That isn't what I meant.
I've lost my sense of scent.
I fear my life is spent.

BOBBY AND LITTLE SALLY:
No one is innocent.

LITTLE SALLY: No one.

(The ghost of BOBBY disappears.)

SOUPY SUE: "No one is innocent"? What did he mean by that?

LITTLE SALLY: I don't know, he started fading in and out after a while. It was a miracle he was alive at all, the fall was so horrible.

TINY TOM: Was he talking about me? How can he say I'm not innocent? Not innocent of what?

LITTLE BECKY TWO-SHOES: Not innocent?! Who the hell does he think he is?!

LITTLE SALLY: Wait! Wait, please. There's more. He said . . . *(She sings.)*

Tell all the people,
Tell them the time is always now.
Tell them to fight for what they know is right.
(The ghost of BOBBY *appears again.)*

BOBBY:
I've lost my sense of sight,
And yet I see them.
I see them standing hand in hand.

BOBBY AND LITTLE SALLY:
I see them standing hand in hand
And cheek to cheek and gland to gland.
There still is hope, I see it, in this land,
If only—

JOSEPHINE: Yes?

BOBBY AND LITTLE SALLY:
If only—

ALL: Yes?!!

LITTLE SALLY: And then he expired.

(The ghost of BOBBY *disappears.)*

LITTLE BECKY TWO-SHOES: The bastard Cladwell lied to us.

JOSEPHINE: He took my Joseph. Now he takes my Bobby.

TINY TOM: Who will lead us now?!

(PENNY enters, unseen.)

SOUPY SUE: We're lost! Lost, I tell you! The rebellion is over!

The Musical

ROBBY THE STOCKFISH: Destroyed with a shove!

TINY TOM: What do we do?!

HOT BLADES HARRY: I'll tell you what we do! We do to her what they did to him!

SOUPY SUE: That's right! Do to her what they did to him!

PENNY: Or you could take me instead.

ALL: Whaa—?!

LITTLE SALLY: Ms. Pennywise!

LITTLE BECKY TWO-SHOES: Seize her!

(THE POOR seize PENNY.)

PENNY: Yes, do whatever you feel you need to, but please, spare the child.

HOT BLADES HARRY: Old woman, you've been grasping and conniving all your days. Why so giving now?

PENNY: Because . . . Hope is my daughter.

ALL: *[Gasp?!]*

PENNY: And I am her mother.

ALL: *[GASP?!!]*

PENNY: Yes, Hope, it's true. I am your mother, the onetime lover of Caldwell B. Cladwell.

TINY TOM: Strumpet!

LITTLE BECKY TWO-SHOES: Slattern!

PENNY: Call me what you will, but it was during the Stink Years, you see. No one thought they had much time then, so many of us did . . . questionable things. There was the looting, of course, and the hoarding. But there were also the fond farewells and the late-night trysts. Life was an explosion filled with riots, cheap cabarets, dancing girls—

LITTLE SALLY: And love?

PENNY: Oh yes, and love. There was love like no tomorrow, for there was no tomorrow, but there is always a tomorrow of some kind or another. After you were born, Caldwell made me promise never to reveal my identity to you, for I was something of a strumpet in my day. *(She removes* HOPE's *gag.)* But never in my wildest—

HOPE: Enough!

ALL: *[Gasp?!]*

HOPE: My heart is telling me many things right now, as you can all well imagine. But one thing it's bellowing louder than anything else is that when there's wrong in the world we must right it. *(She frees herself from her chair.)* You did a wonderful thing by coming here, Ms. Pennywise. Mom. And if you can reform yourself, maybe we can reform a lot more than we know. Ladies and gentlemen of the rebellion, if you want to do to me what they did to Bobby, I wouldn't blame you.

LITTLE BECKY TWO-SHOES: Seize her!

(All move toward HOPE.*)*

HOPE: But if this righteous rebellion were to peter out in Bobby's absence, sending his memory to oblivion, I *would* blame you. All of you! Kill me and the rebellion dies with me. Let me lead you and the rebellion will triumph!

TINY TOM: Lead us?!

ROBBY THE STOCKFISH: She's mad!

HOPE: Lead you to the very nerve center of my father's empire.

PENNY: I've got a key!

HOPE: And the guards know not to question me. But once there, we'll question Daddy. Oh dear, yes, we'll question him plenty!

JOSEPHINE: Why should we trust you?

HOPE: Because Bobby—your hero—loved me. And I loved him.

JOSEPHINE: Hope, dear girl, on behalf of the people of the rebellion, perhaps we, in time, might be able to love you, too.

(They embrace.)

HOPE: It's all that really matters, isn't it? Love? Now let's go do to them what they were ultimately going to do to us!

ALL: Hooray!!

(Segue into . . .)

Scene 5

Montage. HOPE, PENNY, *and* THE POOR *move out to seize UGC headquarters.* LITTLE SALLY *sings.*

LITTLE SALLY:
With a lust for
Saving water,
Man gives daughter
Up for dead!

HOT BLADES HARRY:
Play it on your
Stradivari!
He's not sorry,
Not a shred!

HOPE AND CO.:
He's not sorry . . .
He's not sorry . . .
He's not sorry . . .
He's not sorry . . .

(A street corner: LOCKSTOCK *and* BARREL *enter.)*

BARREL: An absolute maze, that's what the sewer system is.

LOCKSTOCK: I'm going back down to give it another look. You stay here to guard the streets.

*(*HOPE AND CO. *creep into position unnoticed by the* COPS.*)*

BARREL: I've been meaning to ask, Mister Lockstock. Do you ever . . . have doubts about what we've been doing? About the killings and all?

LOCKSTOCK: It may surprise you to learn that sometimes I do, but the health and security of this town are my primary concerns. I love the people of this community, Mister Barrel. Very much. Cladwell's edicts may be their only chance.

(Pause.)

BARREL: And I love you. Very much.

(Pause.)

LOCKSTOCK: I see. *(He exits.)*

BARREL: Well, that went pretty well.

(HOPE AND CO. pounce on BARREL, killing him. JOSEPHINE sings.)

JOSEPHINE:
You who fly the
Blimp of evil,
Shun upheaval
In the air!

SOUPY SUE:
Then ask why the
Ride gets jarry—
Now you're sorry
You're up there.

HOPE AND CO.:
Now you're sorry . . .
Now you're sorry . . .
Now you're sorry . . .
Now you're sorry . . .

(Just outside the UGC headquarters building: FIPP enters, followed by MRS. MILLENNIUM. HOPE AND CO. creep into position.)

FIPP: I'm perfectly capable of finding my own way to the Legislature, you know.

MRS. MILLENNIUM: No offense, Senator, but Mister Cladwell didn't want you flying the coop, what with the coming crackdown and all.

FIPP: And what if I am flying the coop?! What if I'm actually on my way to the airport right now to catch the last flight out to Rio?! What would you say to that?! Hmmm?!

MRS. MILLENNIUM: Can I come?

(HOPE AND CO. sing as they pounce on FIPP and MRS. MILLENNIUM, killing them.)

HOPE AND CO.:

Those who made dough
From debasing
Need erasing,
Need the knife!

Let their blood flow
Like Campari!
We're not sorry—
Hey, that's life!
(Dance break: HOPE AND CO. *sneak through the streets of the city toward UGC headquarters;* CLADWELL *and* MCQUEEN *return from the crackdown;* LOCKSTOCK *and the ghosts of* BARREL, FIPP, *and* MILLENNIUM *enter. All sing.)*

HOPE AND CO.:

Once they liked to
Shoot their rifles,
Just for trifles,
Hunt us down.

CLADWELL AND CO.:

We're not sorry!
We're not sorry!
We're not sorry,
We're not sorry now!

ALL:

Ba-dap! Ba-dap!

HOPE AND CO.:

Now it's we who
Play safari.

CLADWELL AND CO.:

Sorry!
We're not sorry!
We're not—

CLADWELL AND CO.:

We're not sorry!

HOPE AND CO.:

They're not sorry.

BILLY BOY BILL:

I'm not sorry!

ALL:

No one's sorry.

No one's sorry,

Till they get to Urine—

(LOCKSTOCK *and the ghosts exit. The executive offices of UGC:* CLADWELL *and* MCQUEEN *enter.* HOPE AND CO. *are already waiting there, hidden.*)

CLADWELL: Any word from Lockstock and Barrel, Mister McQueen?

MCQUEEN : Not yet, sir. They're still searching the sewer system.

CLADWELL: Which is where they'll be keeping Hope, I imagine. I only pray that when we meet in heaven she can find it in the vastness of her heart to forgive me.

(HOPE *reveals herself.*)

HOPE: Giving up on me so soon, Daddy?

CLADWELL AND MCQUEEN: Whaa—?!

MCQUEEN : Ms. Cladwell, what an unexpected surprise.

HOPE: Is there any other kind?

CLADWELL: Hope, darling, thank God you're safe.

HOPE: I'm not safe yet, Daddy, but I will be. Soon all the people of this land will be safe.

(PENNY *reveals herself.*)

PENNY: Most of us, anyway.

CLADWELL AND MCQUEEN: WHAA—?

PENNY: It's all over, Caldwell. We've come to take you away.

(*The rest of* THE POOR *reveal themselves.*)

CLADWELL: Take me away? But . . . to where?

SOUPY SUE: To the same place you sent young Bobby.

ROBBY THE STOCKFISH: And Old So-and-So.

TINY TOM: And all those who wouldn't—or couldn't—meet your criminal fee hikes.

JOSEPHINE: Seize him!

(THE POOR seize CLADWELL.)

CLADWELL: Hope darling, what's the meaning of this?

HOPE: I've joined the revolution, Daddy. And you? I believe it's time you joined the ex-pat community—in Urinetown!

ALL: *[Gasp!]*

CLADWELL: You're making a terrible mistake, Hope darling. You need me more than you know.

HOPE: The only thing we need now is freedom, Daddy. For the people.

LITTLE SALLY: And love?

HOPE: Oh, yes. And love.

CLADWELL: That's what I used to think, too, Hope. Before the Stink Years. But worldwide ecological devastation has a way of . . . changing a man. You're too young to understand it now, Hope dear, but there really are things more important than love. Food, water, and shelter, for example.

PENNY: And piles and piles of cash?

CLADWELL: It wasn't just cash, Ms. Pennywise. It was an awful lot of cash.

(They sing.)

CLADWELL:
So long, power!

So long, money.

PENNY:

Mister Cladwell,

Caldwell Cladwell.

CLADWELL:
I'm the bunny
This time round.

PENNY:
Remember when our
Nights were starry?

CLADWELL:

Aren't ya sorry?

PENNY:

Sure, I'm sorry.

CLADWELL:

I'm not sorry.

CLADWELL AND PENNY:

Just unsound.

HOPE: Take him away.

(ROBBY THE STOCKFISH *and* BILLY BOY BILL *lead* CLADWELL *out.)*

CLADWELL: I regret nothing! You hear me? Nothing!! Maybe I was a bad father and a cruel and vicious man! But I kept the pee off the street and the water in the ground! You hear me?! I kept the water in the ground!!!

(CLADWELL *is thrown off the roof.* MCQUEEN *tries to exit quietly but is stopped.* ROBBY *and* BILLY *return.)*

MCQUEEN : What now, Ms. Cladwell?

HOPE: Now is the beginning for all of us. Now is a new day when each of us, regardless of race, creed, class, or criminal history, can come together as one people and share the fruits of our labor as one. Now is the dawning of a new age of compassion and the right to do whatever you like, whenever you like, with whomever you like, in whatever location you like. Ladies and gentlemen, today marks the final day of an age of fear, an age that lasted far too long. Today marks the first day of a new age! A new age—

TINY TOM: Don't say it!

HOPE: Of hope! *(She sings.)*

I see a river flowing for freedom.

I see a river just in view.

I see a river flowing for freedom.

I see a river straight and true.

Come to the river flowing for justice.
Come to the river rendezvous.
Come to the river flowing for justice.
All for the people, me and you.
(All scurry about, transforming the UGC of today into the UGC of tomorrow. OFFICER LOCKSTOCK *enters to address the audience directly.)*

LOCKSTOCK: Well, as you guessed, Hope took over her father's business, instituting a series of reforms that opened the public bathrooms to all the people, to pee for free whenever they liked, as much as they liked, for as long as they liked, with whomever they liked. The UGC was renamed the Bobby Strong Memorial Toilet Authority and was operated as a public trust for the benefit of the public.

LITTLE SALLY: Officer Lockstock? Where'd you go?

LOCKSTOCK: Just keeping my head down, Little Sally. Something you should learn to do.

LITTLE SALLY: But aren't you scared the rebels will see you?

LOCKSTOCK: Oh, I may be a cop, but I'm also the narrator. So no one can touch me, not if they want the show to end.

HOPE: So many people peeing at will. Thanks to the Rebellion the world is a much better place.

MCQUEEN : Actually, Ms. Cladwell, your father commissioned a study of water consumption just before he—

HOPE: My father was a tyrant. We need never fear him again. Justice is the only tyrant we need obey.

*(*LITTLE BECKY TWO-SHOES *and* HOPE *sing.)*

LITTLE BECKY TWO-SHOES:
Sisters and brothers, fight for the river.

HOPE:
Fathers and mothers—

LITTLE BECKY TWO-SHOES:
Babies, too!

HOPE AND LITTLE BECKY TWO-SHOES:
All in the family, push toward the river,
Shove toward the river, why don't you?

ALL:
Step in the river, wade in the river,
Soak in the river through and through!
Once in the river, you are the river.
Friends on the shoreline jump in, too.

LOCKSTOCK: Of course, it wasn't long before the water turned silty, brackish, and then disappeared altogether. As cruel as Caldwell B. Cladwell was, his measures effectively regulated water consumption, sparing the town the same fate as the phantom Urinetown. Hope chose to ignore the warning signs, however, preferring to bask in the people's love for as long as it lasted.

LITTLE SALLY: What kind of musical is this?! The good guys finally take over and then everything starts falling apart?!

LOCKSTOCK: Like I said, Little Sally, this isn't a happy musical.

LITTLE SALLY: But the music's so happy!

(LOCKSTOCK chuckles.)

LOCKSTOCK: Yes, Little Sally. Yes, it is.

JOSEPHINE: Such a fever. If only I had a cool, tall glass of water, maybe I'd have a fighting chance.

HOPE: But don't you see, Mrs. Strong? The glass of water's inside you; it always has been.

JOSEPHINE: It has?

HOPE: Of course, it has. Don't you know what you are?

JOSEPHINE: A river?

HOPE: That's right. We all are. *(She sings.)*
You are the river, I am the river.
He is the river, she is, too.

HOPE AND JOSEPHINE:
All are the river flowing for freedom,

Flowing for justice, let's review.
(The ghosts of BOBBY, BARREL, FIPP, *and* CLADWELL *enter.)*

ALL:
We see a river flowing for freedom.
We see a river just in view.
You see a river flowing for freedom.
You see a river straight and true.

LITTLE SALLY: I don't think too many people are going to come see this musical, Officer Lockstock.

LOCKSTOCK: Why do you say that, Little Sally? Don't you think people want to be told that their way of life is unsustainable?

LITTLE SALLY: That—and the title's awful. Can't we do a happy musical next time?

LOCKSTOCK: If there is a next time, I'm sure we can. Well, that's our story. Hope eventually joined her father in a manner not quite so gentle. Mister McQueen opened a bottling factory just outside Brasília, which did rather well until the Amazon dried up. Then he moved. As for the people of this town? They did as best they could. But they were prepared for the world they inherited, weaned as they were on the legend born of their founding father's scare tactics. For when the water dried up, they recognized their town for the first time for what it really was. What it was always waiting to be.

ALL:
This is Urinetown!
Always it's been Urinetown!
This place, it's called Urinetown!

LOCKSTOCK: Hail, Malthus!

ALL: Hail, Malthus!

LOCKSTOCK: Thank you. And good night.

ALL:
That was our show!

In the moments before the Tony broadcast began, a man strolled onstage to read the bejeweled and/or black-tied nominees the riot act. Winners would be allowed one minute from the moment their names were announced to say their piece. Should they be fortunate enough to be invited to do so, winners should make their way quickly to the stage, not thank their babysitter, and get off the stage before the "get off the stage" music started. I heard rumors to this effect in the days leading up to the event and had written a thank-you speech that morning just in case. Read at a comfortable pace, it came in at fifty-eight seconds. Given more time, I would have thanked all the people whose efforts made *Urinetown* possible, including those listed below; to see their names is to know how truly collaborative the making of a musical must be:

Our genius-like, incomparable, stupendous, original Broadway/Off-Broadway cast, including David Beach, Bill Buell, Dwayne Clark, Jennifer Cody, Rachell Coloff, Rick Crom, John Cullum, John Deyle, Hunter Foster, Victor W. Hawks, Erin Hill, Ken Jennings, Spencer Kayden, Megan Lawrence, Stacie Morgain Lewis, Daniel Marcus, Jeff McCarthy, Nancy Opel, Michele Ragusa, Peter Reardon, Don Richard, Lawrence E. Street, Jennifer Laura Thompson, Kay Walbye, and Kirsten Wyatt, all brought together by the casting directors Laura Stanczyk, Jay Binder, and Cindi Rush.

Our steady and extraordinary Broadway/Off-Broadway musicians, including Ed Goldschneider, Paul Garment, Ben Herrington, Tim McLafferty, and Dick Sarpola, all brought together by the music coordinator John Miller.

Our supremely fabulous stage managers, theater managers, and crew, including Julia P. Jones, Matthew Lacey, Joseph R. Bowerman, Sally Campbell Morse, Robert C. Strickstein, Marc Borsak, J. Anthony Magner, Kai Brothers, Susan Bell, Tech Production Services Inc., Joseph Maher, Paul and Andrew Dean, Valarie LaMourt, Elspeth Appleby, Shannon Koger, Megan Rhoads, Lucas Stoffel, George Amores, Mary Mulligan, Todd McKim, William Register, Bobby Driggers, and Dean Gardner.

Our magnificent and many-handed creative team, including John Rando, John Carrafa, Edward Strauss, Bruce Coughlin, Scott Pask, the late, great Jonathan Bixby, Gregory Gale, Brian MacDevitt, Jeff Curtis, Lew Meade, Rick Sordelet, Darlene Dannenfelser, David Kennedy, Jeannine Sabo, Michele Lynch, Orit Jacoby Carroll, Michele Wynne, Gretchen Krich, Yael Lubetzky, and Charles Vorce.

Our visionary, pathfinding, fear-destroying producing team, including Michael David, Lauren Mitchell, Edward Strong, and everyone at Dodger Theatricals, Dodger Marketing, and the Dodger Management Group; TheaterDreams, Inc.; and Michael Rego, Matthew Rego, Hank Unger, Clint Bond, Jr., Aaron Harnick, Jimmy Pellechi, Taylor McGowan, and everyone at the Araca Group.

Our expert and professional boosters of every stripe, including Adrian Bryan-Brown, Jim Byk, Bill Craver, Ben Feldman, Martine Sainvil, Mark Stevenson, and the fine people of Serino Coyne.

Our snowbound yet indomitable January 2000 staged reading crew, including James Barbour, Nancy Opel, Marcus Lovett, Spencer Kayden, Jennifer Laura Thompson, Brooks Ashmanskas, Dale Hensley, Nanci Gaye Bradshaw, Christopher Murney, Tom Gualtieri, Jessica Frankel, Debra Wiseman, Raquel Hecker, Duane Martin Foster, Michael St. John, and Daniel Marcus, all brought together by the casting director Cindi Rush.

Our heroic, utterly unforgettable cast, crew, and creative team from the 1999 New York International Fringe Festival production, including Jay Rhoderick, Spencer Kayden, Wilson Hall, Louise Rozett, Adam Grant, Carol Hickey, Victor Khodadad, Rob Maitner, Terry Cosentino, Nick Balaban, Kristen Anderson, Bellavia Mauro, Zachary Lasher, Allison Schubert, Raquel Hecker, Joseph P. McDonnell, Wylie Goodman, Karen Flood, Michael Stuart, Peggotty Roecker, and Jane Charlotte Jones.

The gratitude-inducing forces behind the New York International Fringe Festival, including John Clancy and Elena K. Holy.

The prescient collection of actors and theater practitioners who first perused the script, sang the songs, and read the lines, all in the name of improving the material, including Andy Cook, Steven Singer, Nannette Deasy, Debra Wassum, Eric Carrillo, Jim Andralis, Raven Snook, Ian W. Hill, Adrienne Asterita, Dann B. Black, Heidi Godt, Alana Israelson, Dan Perry, Marcus Woollen, David Auburn, Scott Hermes, Bob Fisher, Tommy Moore, Stan Schwartz, Diana Slickman, Greg Allen, Robert Stockfish, Bill and Rob Coelius, and Sean Bosker.

Pastor Brooke Swertfager and the congregation of Christ Lutheran Church in Manhattan.

Co-workers past and present, including the good people of the Neo-Futurists, and the really very good people of the Cardiff Giant Theater Company.

And, ultimately, our own community of friends and family members who have made this life of writing plays possible, including Paula Kotis, Sam Kotis, Juanita and Ray Hollmann, Jilly Perlberger, and, finally, Ayun Halliday, who made us keep going even when we didn't want to.

Thank you.

GREG KOTIS AND MARK HOLLMANN